D1711367

Rediscovering the South's Celtic Heritage

The Overmountain Press

JOHNSON CITY, TENNESSEE

Acknowledgments

~~~~~~

I must give strong thanks to a number of people who have in one way or another shaped my perspectives, research skills, and motivation to write or finish this book. Professors Frank "Pete" Charton, Harriman, Tennessee; Barbara E. Hinton, Fayetteville, Arkansas; Conrad T. Moore, Bowling Green, Kentucky; and Gilbert Fernandez, Cookeville, Tennessee. I also want to thank Professors Howard Hotson at the University of Aberdeen; Jane Ohlmeyer at Trinity College—Dublin; Ian Haslett, University of Glasgow; and especially Drs. A. W. "Tony" Parker and Alan MacDonald at the University of Dundee for helping me to embrace historical methodologies. I also thank Dr. Parker for employing me as an honorary teaching fellow at the University of Dundee. Further thanks are due to the Rev. Colin Williamson, Church of Scotland. Professors Ceri Peach at Oxford University and Nicholas Canny at National University of Ireland-Galway are appreciated for encouraging the continuance of my research. I am especially grateful to Dr. Richard M. Smith, Director of the Cambridge University Group for the History of Population and Social Structure, for taking me under his tutelage as I investigate the Plantation of Ulster and the trans-channel evolution of a Protestant-Scots community.

As a Native of East Tennessee with Scots, Irish, Welsh, English, and French ancestry (each well represented in Ulster), I am forever grateful to my mother, Dorothy Jones, and grandmother, Vernedith "Nanny" Voyles. May their storytelling abilities continue to live in this book. I also want to thank my father, Harry Mac Vann Jr., for his dedication to heritage preservation. A deep debt is owed to Sandy Vann, and I want to thank my children, Sarah and Preston, for their patience and love during the writing of this book. Finally, the help provided to me by Jason Weems at The Overmountain Press in turning the academic jargon of the original manuscript into something resembling English is much appreciated. While I acknowledge the valuable help I have received from these people in shaping my thoughts and approach to writing this book, any errors or faulty interpretations are exclusively mine.

This book is dedicated to Steven Daniel Bailey, my lifelong friend whose gifts will never be realized.

Table of Contents

⊚⊚⊚⊚⊚⊚⊚⊚⊚⊚⊚⊚⊚⊚⊚⊚⊚⊚⊚⊚⊚⊚⊚⊚⊚⊚⊚⊚⊚⊚⊚⊚⊚⊚⊚⊚

Introduction

@@

In the 18th century, a passionate, independent people from the Celtic fringes of the British Isles streamed into Appalachia like floodwaters over the banks of a swollen river. They came from remote upland areas of Wales, northern and western England, Scotland, and Ireland, but the souls Patrick Griffin called "the people with no name," the Scotch-Irish, made the crest of settlers rise over the Appalachian mountains and spill into the Mississippi Valley and beyond.

The Celtic people saw political, economic, and religious freedom come together for the first time in their small mountain communities in Appalachia. Their ancestors from the British Isles and northwestern Europe had not been free since the Normans introduced feudalism into Scotland during the 12th century. Economic freedom and political independence were cherished by the Celts.

The remoteness of the ridges and valleys of Appalachia insured the preservation of economic and political relationships that were learned in Northern Ireland. It was difficult to get into the region, and it was certainly difficult to get out. In addition to self-reliance, the region preserved other cultural traits that have been attributed to the Scotch-Irish, including fatalism, insecurity, belief in natural liberty, a deep need for religion, and a tendency to emphasize the supernatural.

When one examines America's Celtic hearth (Appalachia and the Ozarks) and the literature written about the land and its people, it becomes clear that most writers recognize the uniqueness of the culture but fail to see the Celtic connection. The language, music, food, clothing, and religious beliefs of many Appalachian and Ozark folk—including those who migrated in large numbers to Mississippi, Kansas, Texas, and Oklahoma—are, in part, products of cultural roots that began centuries ago in a profoundly similar, but far-removed, place.

By preserving their culture, the early settlers had a way to remember their loved ones who remained across the ocean, including those who had long since been laid to rest in the glens and moorlands of Scotland and Ireland. While the words *Scotland* and *Ulster* do not often flow from the mouths of Southern highlanders, the ways of the Old World survive in many remote parts of America's Southern highlands.

European History and Southern Culture

〰〰〰〰〰〰〰〰〰〰〰〰〰〰〰〰〰〰〰〰〰〰〰〰〰〰〰〰〰〰〰〰

Some of America's most scenic areas lie in the Southern highlands between southwestern Pennsylvania and eastern Oklahoma. Like a skilled surgeon, the Mississippi River and its fertile plain cut in half this belt of rugged tree-covered ridges and stream-carved valleys. The mighty Mississippi, however, could not wash away the migration route of land-hungry settlers from Southern Appalachia.

During the 18th and 19th centuries, brave pioneers and their families advanced across this belt of southern plains and uplands, creating the cultural region we know as the Upland South. Their arrival in the backcountry was not achieved for the sake of fame or riches, though economic freedom was an important reason. The hilly and mountainous landscape provided the pioneers with an opportunity to live according to their own dreams and plans, ideas that were often regulated or determined by spiritual considerations.

Despite their newly acquired freedom from Europe's last vestiges of feudalism, the pioneers tightly held on to many of their Old World ways. In fact, the isolation created by the Upland South's mountains, valleys, and plateaus has helped to preserve many of the ethnic traits that have long since disappeared from the pioneers' European homelands. The hill and mountain culture of the South is, therefore, a window through which to rediscover a world that predates Columbus's oceanic crossing by many centuries.

The South's culture, especially in the highland areas of Appalachia and the Ozarks, has been greatly influenced by the Celtic Christians who emigrated from Ireland and the British highlands, as well as from the Germanic states of northwestern Europe. Their contribution to the cultural makeup of America can be appreciated from both a geographic and a historic perspective. For example, as the descendants of Appalachia's Celtic people moved westward, building homesteads, churches, and schools along the way, they created the Upland South's culture. They were especially fond of settling in isolated and rugged places like the Little Ozarks of Kansas and the Texas Hill Country.

Most of the folkways of the Upland South are continuations of cultural practices that have their roots in Roman Britain, pre-Viking Denmark (Juteland), and Reformation Switzerland. The ethnic backgrounds of white Southerners have often been ignored in explanations of the South's economic and social development. Religion is frequently used to define the region, which is known as the "Bible Belt." Divorcing the people's religious beliefs from their ethnic background leads to some fundamental misunderstandings about the region. The power of the Southern church today is similar in significance to the institution established by the first settlers. As it was in 1750, the Southern house of worship is an important part of the continuing Celtic way of life.

Religion, however, is only part of a cultural world that has survived nearly 300 years of poverty, out-migration, and prejudice. In addition to those threats, today the Upland South's culture is under siege from within, as non-Southerners move into the region and create a suburban way of life. Many new residents are seasonal or second homeowners. Their demand for housing has driven up the cost of home ownership, a bane for many of the poorest residents. In light of the threats to the ancient and persevering culture of the region, this book, by recognizing its history and its rightful place in America's cultural mosaic, endeavors to help us rediscover the Celtic folkways that make the Upland South unique.

Celtic Influence on Backcountry Christianity

The number of Presbyterian-affiliated colleges based on Calvinist or Reformed doctrines in the Upland South is evidence of the impact of early Scotch-Irish pioneers. Scotch-Irish settlers from Ulster (the nine northernmost counties in Ireland) brought their faith with them to the New World. The Scotch-Irish people are Celts whose ancestors include Vikings, Angles, Irish Gaels, and Britons. They, like most Western Europeans, were swept up in the Protestant Reformation that began in the early 16th century.

The Scotch-Irish Celts accepted the Calvinist teachings of John Knox, who wanted to educate people to read scripture. In Knox's way of thinking, the clergy had to be exceptionally educated, for they served as the clerics and teachers of their flocks. Literacy was important, because the Creator chose to reveal Himself to a fallen and depraved people through the spoken and written Word of God. Colleges were necessary for the preparation of ministers in the Church of Scotland (Kirk), which officially replaced the Roman Catholic Church of Scotland following the Scottish Reformation.

The establishment of colleges in America's backcountry provided learning opportunities for a limited number of frontier lads. Among the new Presbyterian colleges were Hampden Sydney and Mary Baldwin colleges in Virginia, Davidson College in North Carolina, and Franklin College, which began in 1800 and later grew into the University of Georgia. In Tennessee, the work of Samuel Doak, a Presbyterian minister, helped to make higher learning possible in the area. The predecessors of the University of Tennessee were Presbyterian colleges. Tusculum College, established in 1794 in Greeneville, Tennessee, is one of the oldest colleges west of the Blue Ridge Mountains. Later Presbyterians established Pikeville College in Kentucky, Lees-McRae and St. Andrew's colleges in North Carolina, Lyon College in Arkansas, Belhaven College in Mississippi, and the University of Tulsa in Oklahoma.

Despite the number of early Presbyterian colleges in the Upland South, the size of the population far exceeded the Church's ability to provide worship services on Sundays and taxed the resources needed to educate teachers for remote communities in desperate need of literacy skills. Many Presbyterians grew to maturity with no formal education. For those who wished to join a congregation, their choices in worship style and theology were extremely limited.

The congregations that grew during the late colonial days, however, were typically independent, spiritual, and disinterested in intellectual discussions about theology. Many pastors were illiterate and relied upon God for "insight." Sermons were, at best, grounded in a theology in which God was judicial, loving, and continually self-revealing through dreams and other spiritual manifestations.

Like the progeny of Scotch-Irish Presbyterians, the descendants of Germanic Mennonites, Amish, and Moravian settlers of Pennsylvania came to the backcountry with spiritual longings and certain fundamental beliefs. As Christians on the frontier, they were not members of any denomination as we think of them today. Because these settlers followed a doctrine of believer baptism, they were called *Anabaptists*, which means *rebaptizer,* because in the old country most adults had already been baptized as infants. It is perhaps better to think of them as communities of faith that introduced the sacrament of believer baptism into Southern Appalachian culture.

The fertile valley lands of the Appalachian backcountry beckoned to the Anabaptists as their families grew, and, like the Scotch-Irish, their need for survival pushed them westward to the Shenandoah Valley and then southward into Southern Appalachia. They, like the Scotch-Irish Presbyterians, practiced spirit-filled worship and believed in the separation of church and state. With the exception of infant baptism and education requirements for their clergy, which was a serious factor limiting the spread of Presbyterianism into the farthest reaches of the colonial backcountry, the Scotch-Irish had much in common with their Celtic cousins from the old country. Through commingling and intermarrying with the Scotch-Irish, the South's uniquely conservative, yet expressive, form of worship gave birth to several Baptist associations, including the Old Regular Baptists in 1825 and the Southern Baptist Convention that was formed in 1845.

The Roman scholar Strabo wrote about the Germani (Germans) who lived in the lands east of the Rhine River. In Latin, *Germani* means authentic, or pure-type. In Strabo's mind, the Germani were the purest of the Celts. They were taller, blonder, and more fierce than their cousins in the British Isles. Culturally, they were like all Celts, passionate and undisciplined with a flair for creativity in both speech and the arts. Celtic art reached its highest level of achievement between 500 B.C. and 50 B.C.

In 1857, archeologists working at a site called La Tène, on the northern shores of Lake Neuchatel in Switzerland, made a discovery that yielded a wealth of artifacts from the height of Celtic society, including swords, spearheads, tools, and shields of brilliant artistry. Representations of plants, animals, and spiral patterns were the basic forms used in their art, a style known today as *La Tène*. Examples of La Tène art have been found throughout the Celtic lands of Europe. The Celts' passion for descriptive words is also a product of their creative, freedom-loving dispositions and may have contributed to the Protestant Reformation during the 16th century.

The post-Luther Reformation, including the Anabaptist movement, was started in the Germanic lands of modern-day

Switzerland. John Calvin, for whom Calvinism is named, worked out his ideas about church government and theology in Geneva. So, did the independent qualities of the Celtic people in the southern Germanic states help to bring about the Protestant Reformation? In Scotland, a nation with deep Celtic roots, the Reformation was born by will of the people. In England, however, it was ushered in by the will and power of the monarch Henry VIII.

Consider the fact that in the 16th century an autocratic, monopolistic Roman Catholic Church was supported by the Holy Roman Empire, a territorial power that was seldom Roman and rarely holy. Also, consider the replacement of popes, cardinals, bishops, and priests with the self as a medium for communicating with God. An open dialogue between God and self is the basis for a truly independent religious experience, which is a fundamental part of the Celtic lifestyle. It is important to remember that the ancestors of these religious revolutionaries were Strabo's Germani. Their descendants became part of America's Southern backcountry settlers.

Free from rigid church-state discipline, the Scotch-Irish in the American backcountry sought communion with others who shared their need for self-determination in a world controlled by a God whose rule was absolute, but whose love was limitless.

Regional Prejudices in Britain Transplanted to America

Attitudes about religion and the Church were not the only dispositions imported to the colonies from the British Isles. Regional identities and cultures were brought to North America, along with other ways of life. The differences in America between the North and the South, which continue to play a major role in national politics and regional prejudices, have their roots in Britain.

Many of the pioneers who settled in Southern Appalachia were from Ulster, but their ancestors were from the Scottish

Ulster-American Folk Park, County Tyrone, Northern Ireland

Lowlands and northern England. They were not descendants of Saxons or southern English nobles. The northern, or border, English descended from Angles, Britons, Irish Gaels, and Norse Vikings. The southern English who settled in America's northern colonies, however, descended from a Brythonic Celtic tribe, Romans, Frisians from northern Holland, Saxons from northern Germany, Jutes from northern Denmark, and Normans. Although there is little evidence, it is likely that the original inhabitants of the British Isles, who are thought to have emigrated from the Mediterranean region, are also ancestors of the people in southern Britain.

Regional differences and biases in America can be traced to cultural disparities first created by Romans in Britain during the era of the Republic. The most important Roman contributions to southern England included roads and towns such as Winchester and London. Several centuries later, the Normans took advantage of the roads and towns created by the Romans and further developed southern England. The Normans, however, did not expend the same effort to develop the impover-

7

Shenandoah Valley, Virginia

ished lands of northern England, Ireland, Scotland, and Wales.

When settlers from southern England arrived in the New World, they created the colonies that became New England. Emigrants from the impoverished northern England and the other Celtic lands of Ireland, Scotland, and Wales became the largest ethnic group to settle in Southern Appalachia. The culture of Southern Appalachia is, therefore, based on that of the Celtic lands of the British Isles and, to some extent, on the culture of the Germanic tribes of northwestern Europe. The culture of New England, however, grew out of the relatively more advanced southern part of England.

Emigration from the Old World

During the 18th century, less than 100 years after leaving Scotland and settling in Ulster, Ulster-Scots left their homes by the tens of thousands because of political and religious persecution. (The fourth and twelfth chapters provide a more complete discussion on the factors that led to Ulster-Scots emigration.) Most of the landlords in Ulster were residents and citizens of England. They had little concern for those who labored on their farms and in their mills. The landlords raised rents beyond the ability of their tenants to pay, which is called *rack-renting*. It was a contributing factor in the 18th-century Ulster emigration, as it would be during the migration forced by the Potato Famine of the mid-19th century.

Settling Southern Appalachia

Although Ulster Protestants, upon immigrating to the New World, were comparatively better off than their counterparts who remained in Scotland and northern England, most were able to pay only their ship's passage, and many had little with which to homestead. A number of them were unable to pay their way across the ocean, so they became indentured servants when they arrived in port. Others became squatters on the frontier and never actually paid for their land. The vast majority of the Scotch-Irish immigrants did not linger in urban areas such as Philadelphia or Charleston. Most purchased supplies and headed out to the frontier. For the land-seeking Scotch-Irish immigrant, there was no time for assimilation into American colonial society.

The Scotch-Irish settler along Virginia's Great Wagon Road was seldom involved with commercial agriculture. Scotch-Irish farmers and their families faced tremendous, but familiar, hardships. For most of their history they had been subjected to extreme poverty, with little chance for improvement. Except for what they had learned in Ulster about economic freedom and personal achievement, the mind-set of the Scotch-Irish in Appalachia was only a few generations removed from the knowledge and attitudes of the Middle Ages.

Northern Ireland did not create a class of social-climbing entrepreneurs like those who would form the basis of the plantation society in America's Deep South. Instead, the Scotch-Irish who arrived in the backcountry of the Carolinas, Georgia, Tennessee, and Kentucky were a mostly poor people who depended on family for support and friendship and relied on subsistence agriculture to survive.

In Ulster, northern English, like the Scots, were living on confiscated lands formerly occupied by Gaelic-speaking Irish clans. The Scots and the English were left to socialize with each other, encouraging a common cultural identity among their descendants, including those in Southern Appalachia. Together, the Ulster-Scots and the northern English, upon arriving in Appalachia, formed the Scotch-Irish lifestyle. The burgeoning culture quickly adopted isolated settlers of Huguenot-French and Welsh descent. A common Celtic heritage greatly facilitated the assimilation of Welsh settlers, while the Calvinistic faith of the French eased their acceptance into the Scotch-Irish world.

Germanic peoples composed the second-largest group on the frontier. They came to North America from the regions presently located in southern Germany and Switzerland. Their reasons for emigrating from Europe, like the Ulster-Scots, were primarily rooted in the religious persecution and political instability that defined their homeland experience. Generally speaking, most of the Germanic peoples, including the Swiss, were Anabaptists or Calvinists who readily interacted with the more numerous Scotch-Irish settlers. They followed a similar migration route as the Scotch-Irish and often settled on farmsteads at nearby locations.

Unlike the Scotch-Irish, the Germans were excellent farmers and artisans in their new environment. Being pacifists who considered armed conflict unnecessary to maintain Christian lives, the Anabaptists chose vulnerable homesites because they were located in fertile valleys. They were also adept at applying manure as a fertilizer. The Scotch-Irish, on the other hand, often cleared homesites on less fertile but strategic ridgetops that offered better protection in the event of Indian attacks.

The Germans had little contact with groups other than the Scotch-Irish, so they learned the English dialect that was spoken in Ulster and the Border Region of Great Britain. The Anabaptists preferred an orderly life without conflict with their neighbors, including Indians. The Scotch-Irish, however, seemed determined to quarrel with the native folk. The fierce and quarrelsome disposition of the Scotch-Irish probably resulted from centuries of insecurity acquired while living on the border of England and in Ulster. In America, their dispositions were reinforced on the frontier, where they acted as the European vanguard against various Native American tribes.

Roots of Southern Appalachian Poverty and Insecurity

Insecurity and impoverishment among the Ulster immigrants was partly caused by a reliance on the feudal-clan system and its slow death in the Border Region. Though the northern English and Lowland Scots are uniquely different ethnic groups, they have almost the same ancestors. The Irish Gaels, however, were a stronger cultural force upon the Lowland Scots than they were upon the northern English.

The English lived in a geographic region that was similar in location, terrain, and climate to that of the Lowland Scots, and their possession of technology used to harness a living from the environment was not much more advanced than that of their Scottish counterparts. Lairds (lords) in the border country were slowly renting out lands to the highest bidder in a scheme called a *feu*. The feu, which began in the 16th century, was a device which displaced many peasant farm families whose very lives had depended on their feudal lord for security and support in exchange for service. The effect of the feu was made worse by intense famine in the late 1690s. By 1699, as many as one-third to one-half of the Scottish population had either died or had emigrated.

Living on opposite sides of the disputed border between Scotland and England was the most significant factor in the formation of the differing cultures of the Lowland Scots and the northern English. The English and the Scots fought over the region for nearly four centuries. Moreover, because Norman nobles were given lands in both England and Scotland, a feudal-clan system evolved and prevailed around the border.

View of the Ozark Mountains

Feudalism, however, did not replace the Celtic clan system prevalent in most of Scotland, because the Norman lords represented a small portion of the population. Many of the lords, in fact, lost their Norman identities as they adapted to the culture of the more abundant Scots.

Feudalism made its way into the Scottish Lowlands in the 12th century, as a number of Norman nobles took advantage of an invitation from Scotland's King David I. The king believed that the Normans would help the Scots develop the Lowlands. Over the next two centuries the Normans did not attempt to conquer Scotland, but Norman rule over England galvanized national identities. According to Strong, "The realm of England which the Normans conquered consisted of the lowlands, the south-east and west and the midlands. Beyond these lay the Celtic lands of Wales, Cumberland, and Scotland." These regions, in Celtic fashion, resisted the formation of a strong central government, a trait that remains a political reality in America's Upland South.

In 1274, a new monarch who saw those Celtic lands as part

Stirling Bridge. This bridge crosses the River Forth a few hundred yards from the site where William Wallace stopped the army of England's Edward I.

of his island realm rose to the English throne. Edward I, the Plantagenet family's most capable ruler, began a conquest of the island of Great Britain that first led to the takeover of Wales. Soon afterward, Edward sent his armies into the lands north of England's border, where he hoped to take advantage of the untimely death of Scotland's King Alexander III, but his marauding efforts failed. William Wallace, himself part Norman, defeated a much larger English force at Stirling Bridge at the end of the 13th century. Wallace, the guerrilla fighter who inspired thousands of fellow Scots to take up swords against the English king, was subsequently defeated and humiliated at Falkirk.

Wallace's rapid fall from political power was precipitated by paranoid Scottish nobles from the Lowlands who, despite Wallace's efforts to gain diplomatic help against England during the years that followed Falkirk, saw him as a liability. These same nobles sacrificed Wallace to Edward for a bribe. The English king quickly had Sir William Wallace, the Protector of Scotland, barbarously executed.

Wallace's resistance, however, inspired the more politically astute Robert Bruce to lead a quest for Scottish independence from England at the Battle of Bannockburn, in 1314. By this time, Edward II was England's monarch. His ineptitude greatly contributed to Bruce's victory over a much larger English force. The events set a precedent for strife that would last for nearly 400 years. Bitter conflict raged on both sides of the border as English and Scottish forces conducted a series of military campaigns to capture Scotland's most productive farmlands. Counteroffensives by Scottish forces were mostly acts of vengeance and seldom resulted in the occupation of English soil.

As a result of constant warfare and endemic poverty, banditry became commonplace. The feudal-clan system provided families with a sense of security when faced with bandits, rival clan violence, and foreign adversaries, including their English neighbors across the border. Consequently, the culture of the region produced a person who was insecure, poor, often violent, and heavily dependent upon family members for friendship and support. Faced with a hazardous life, the border peasant became suspicious of anyone who was not kin.

To appreciate the culture of the uplands of Southern Appalachia and the Ozarks, one must consider how, in the early 1600s, King James I, the first monarch to have the power to control events in the war-torn region, brought peace and economic opportunity to the Protestant residents on both sides of the border between England and Scotland.

James I was decisive in dealing with the borderlands. He created order where there was none. He continued Queen Elizabeth's policy of seizing lands in Ulster from its resident Roman Catholics, whom the English thought of as savages. He encouraged Protestants from the borderlands to rent and cultivate farms and woodlands the English government had forcibly taken from their occupants. The resettlement of Protestants on seized lands was called the Plantation of Ulster.

William Wallace Monument, Stirling, Scotland

The overwhelming majority of those who settled in Ulster were from Scotland.

The Protestant settlers in Ulster brought their culture with them, including their sense of insecurity that was developed in the lawless borderlands. The Ulster-Scots now had to deal with hostile neighbors who spoke Gaelic and celebrated Christ in a different house of worship. The Protestant settlers, who were mostly Presbyterian, served as a buffer zone between Protestant England and angry Catholic Ireland.

The bitterness that persists today between Protestants and Catholics in Northern Ireland has its roots in the Plantation Movement. The Ulster-Scots, upon settling in the American backcountry, also served as a buffer zone against Native Americans, who, like the Catholic Irish, were crowded off of their ancestral lands. The Ulster-Scots, now more commonly known as the Scotch-Irish, never had a chance to develop a culture free of hostilities and insecurities.

Celts in the Census

The previous chapter tells us that Southern Appalachia and the Ozarks were, during colonial times, heavily populated by British and Germanic Celtic people, but to what extent have the Celts impacted the population of the entire South? Although the U.S. Bureau of Census has infrequently collected data on white ethnic groups, most sociologists and journalists see white Southerners as part of one common group. Because of that assumption, many writers use a simplistic approach when describing the American population as a whole. For example, Warmenhoven reports that the population of the United States is 80 percent white, 12 percent black, 6 percent Hispanic, and 2 percent Asian. There are also small numbers of Pacific Islanders, Inuits, and Aleuts living in the United States.

The 1990 census data, however, tell us that, of the 254 million people who called the United States their legal country of residence, just over 12 million referred to themselves as "American only." Surprisingly, only 32 million claimed English ancestry, despite the early majority of the southern British in New England and other coastal settlements. In 1990 there were over 159 million whites living in the United States who did not claim English, or American-only, heritage. It is not possible to use the year 2000 Census data because the ques-

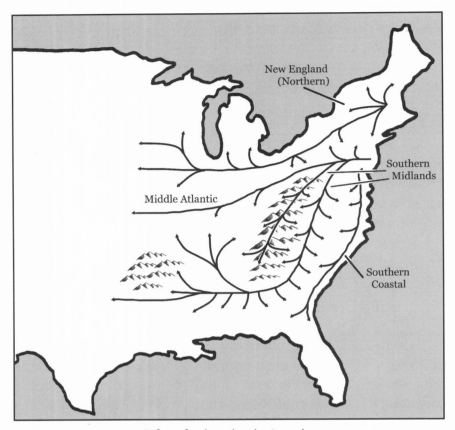

Cultural migration in America

tionnaires did not ask white Americans to select an ethnic nationality.

It is hard to know exactly how many Southerners are of Scots, Scotch-Irish, Irish, Welsh, or English ancestry because of the idea that most white Americans are of English, or Anglo-Saxon, descent. For example, popular authors of college textbooks, such as sociologists Giddens and Kerbo, do not mention any numbers for the Scots and Scotch-Irish or provide any discussion on their ways of life. Tischler, another respected sociologist, does not include any discussion or numbers on the Scotch-Irish, but he does include the Scots and the Welsh under the Anglo-Saxon label and states that there are over 60 million Americans of that ethnicity.

Census data on white ethnic groups are available on a limited basis, but the numbers on a few of them are probably too low to reflect reality. Census numbers on white nationalities, or ethnic groups, were gathered from responses to questions on the 1980 and 1990 censuses. The Census Bureau divides the United States into four regions: Northeast, South, Midwest, and West.

In the 1990 census, 85 percent of Americans cited one or more countries as the source of their ethnic affiliation. Sixty percent of the citizenry who called themselves American-only lived in the Southern region. Also in 1990, 47 percent of America's 5.6 million Scotch-Irish lived in the South.

In 1990 there were 203 million white Americans of European descent living in the United States. The largest ethnic group was German, with 57 million people claiming German lineage. Twenty-five percent of this population lives in the South. Thirty-three percent of the 38 million Irish in America live in areas south of the Ohio River. English descendants numbered 32 million. Thirty-five percent of the people who claim English descent live in the South. There were 5.3 million Scots residing in the United States in 1990, with 1.8 million in the South. There are 549,000 Southerners of Welsh descent, representing 27 percent of the nation's total. As this chapter shows in later sections, the figures for the Scotch-Irish and Scots are too low.

The numbers on non-Germanic Celts (Scotch-Irish, Irish, Scots, and Welsh) tell us this group is the largest white ethnic nationality residing in the South, with 17.5 million people. Germanic peoples compose the second-largest nationality in the South, with 14.3 million people, and the English group is third, with just over 11 million. The English group may include, however, an indeterminable number of Anglo-Celtic descendants from England's Cornwall, Cumbria, and Devonshire, as well as Northumbria. These census numbers tell us that Celtic people have impacted the South. This impact is rendered more apparent when considering that their combined numbers total

31.7 million people. The number of Celts living in the South is comparable to the entire population of African-Americans in the United States.

Explaining the Census Numbers

In the case of the Scotch-Irish population, the following facts explain why the census data are presumably too low. Scotch-Irish settlers were subsistence farmers (field to kitchen) and relied heavily on animal labor for much of the work needed on their Appalachian homesteads. Early settlers, many of whom were devout Calvinists, saw children as blessings because they were a labor source for the farm. There were few, if any, reliable birth control methods, so the rural population grew rapidly and expanded westward across the South. It was not uncommon for a couple to have five or more children.

If the Scotch-Irish averaged a three percent annual natural increase rate (four births per one death), their number would have grown from Leyburn's estimate of 200,000 in the year 1775 to just over 10 million by the outbreak of World War I. This scenario assumes there were no new immigrants from Northern Ireland, and that those here since 1910 only replaced themselves. Because both of these assumptions are unlikely, a more accurate figure for the Scotch-Irish population is probably between 15 million and 20 million, and the Scots number is closer to 10 million. These figures are also cited in the PBS series "The Story of English."

The reason for the low number of people claiming to be Scotch-Irish rests with the fact that many immigrants from Ulster called themselves Irish. These immigrants maintained an Irish identity when Scotch-Irish would have been more accurate. Although most of the immigrants were descendants of Protestant Scots from the Lowlands, or southern half, of Scotland, the generations their families spent in Ireland gave them a new sense of "home."

When they left Ulster, Ireland was the place they missed

and longed for during their treacherous journey across the Atlantic. Irish Celtic music comforted the families' lonely hearts. When they arrived in the colonies, Irish and Scottish whiskey warmed their bones. When they settled among their kin and others, who were often from their Ulster communities, Reformed Presbyterianism reassured them of their place in God's Providence. In the early days of North American settlement, however, most of the Ulstermen simply referred to themselves as Irish, because they had emigrated from Ireland.

Most Irish Protestants began calling themselves Scotch-Irish after Ireland's Potato Famine of the 1840s and early 1850s forced 2,000,000 destitute Irish Catholics to immigrate to the United States. The Protestants wanted to make it clear that they were not to be counted among their poorer Irish cousins. It is likely that many Irish Southerners, who were not threatened by the anti-Irish stigmas concocted by Northern workers, saw little merit in attaching *Scotch* to their Irish identity.

A second reason for such a low figure for the Scotch-Irish in the 1990 Census rests with the number of generations that have passed since the arrival of the earliest Ulster immigrants. Some Scotch-Irish immigrants arrived in the colonies before 1700, but the first great wave occurred in 1717-1718. If four generations are added to those settlers' family trees every 100 years, it produces eight generations of ancestors by 1918, and eleven by 2001! Eight generations of ancestors produce 256 separate surnames, and 11 generations produce 2,048 family names. An ethnic link is easily lost in that ancestral maze! It is quite possible that an 11th-generation Celt may not know the origin of his or her culture. As a result, many Celts have lost their true ethnic identity and conveniently claimed another national label.

John Rice Irwin, proprietor of the Appalachian Museum in Norris, Tennessee, offers a plausible explanation for the loss of the Scotch-Irish identity. He points out that when settlers made their way into Tennessee, they thought of themselves as being from North Carolina or Virginia. Because the early

18th-century settlers were members of a community with an oral tradition, stories about the old country, or the land across the "big water," merged with those of the firstborn of America.

With few exceptions, the early Scotch-Irish settlers easily molded their institutions to fit their new environment, which looked a lot like Ulster and northern Britain. When relating stories of old, they probably communicated the moral without regard to where the events took place. In essence, the Scotch-Irish and other Celts made America their home. Losing connection with the Scotch-Irish and Celtic labels did not mean, however, that they ceased being Celtic in practice or in blood.

Regardless of the difficulties associated with finding genealogical records, we can be reasonably certain that families often migrated with others from their European communities. When they settled together, they unconsciously maintained a Celtic way of life. Caudill, after studying the surnames of Eastern Kentucky, found that most families were of Welsh descent. There may not be many Welsh people in America, but it would appear that, at least in the South, they settled near each other by random chance—which is not likely—or they migrated together. In isolated environments, such as those found in the rural South, the majority ethnic group will assert its culture over any and all minority nationalities.

The blending of national identities and the birth of the Scotch-Irish people occurred in Ulster, but the process was not completed until their settlement in America's Southern highlands. Northern-English immigrants composed a large segment of the total English population on the Appalachian frontier during the 1700s. In Southern Appalachia today, it is difficult to make accurate accounts of national identities. The northern English have joined their Scottish Lowland cousins to become America's Scotch-Irish. For example, Bill and Mary Durning include names such as Creswell and Payne—neither of which are of Scottish or Irish origin—in their list of surnames of "hardy Scotch-Irish pioneers," which they present in

Shenandoah Valley, Virginia

The Scotch-Irish Who Came to America: A Genealogical History. In fact, they are English family names.

After so many years, how can we know what nationality is most accurate for those who live in the Upland South? The next chapter explains how the geography of the Upland South and the care and rearing provided by mothers have preserved the Celtic ways of life.

Culture is a Mother's Gift

Cultural ways may well be the gift of our maternal family lines. Southerners understand words and phrases like *fixin' to*, *skift*, and *you'ns*; sometimes eat cornbread in milk; and are often taught to believe in doctrines such as the Perseverance of the Saints ("once saved always saved"). These examples of Southern culture demonstrate a uniqueness among America's white ethnic groups. In fact, these cultural expressions began hundreds of years ago in the British Highlands and in Switzerland.

In Europe, as in the South, surnames are generally passed along male family lines. Historically, however, the fathers have had little involvement in child care and the teaching of basic culture to their children.

Three hundred years prior to the Vikings' arrival in Britain during the 8th century, other Germanic tribes invaded England and southern Scotland and brought their wives and children with them. As a result of the presence of Anglo wives, their children learned the language of their parents' homeland, the central region of the modern-day country of Denmark. That language formed the basis of the Northumbrian dialect, which became known in America as Southern Midlands speech, the tongue of Southern Appalachia. It would seem, then, that children are more likely to learn most of their culture from their mothers; therefore, maternal lines in a person's family tree are often the source of ethnicity.

Analyzing the surnames of established rural communities, or those surnames spread over larger geographic regions, can provide important information about the ancestors of the people who live in the particular region. Harry Caudill conducted such a study in 1982. In studies like Caudill's, we assume that rural areas experience little in-migration and that the surnames of mothers would probably be among those identified.

The passage of culture from generation to generation is an amazing process, especially when one appreciates the complexity of the system through which it passes. A person has 1,024 males and 1,024 females (2,048 ancestors of the same generation) who are their 9th great grandparents. It is easy to forget that of those 2,048 ancestors that produced your immediate 11 generations, only one was born with the same surname as you! It is possible, of course, that ancestors of the same name married one another.

Are the surnames in a typical Southern Appalachian community Celtic or Anglo-Saxon? The easiest way to find out is to examine the surnames throughout the region. However, it is simply too cumbersome a task to examine the origin of each surname of the people who live in Appalachia. Instead, a small highland community called Sandy Gap, North Carolina, was chosen for a family-name survey. Sandy Gap is located in Cherokee County, North Carolina, and is less than 10 miles from the Georgia and Tennessee state lines. The community was selected for a case study because the area currently faces change, as land developers establish mountain resorts and second homes for nonresident owners.

The following table shows the national origins of 31 family names in the Sandy Gap area. The surnames were part of the Sandy Gap community during the 1930s. Members of each family are still represented in the area. National categories were identified through comments made by community members. The names they provided were then cross-referenced in Black's *Surnames of Scotland: Their Origin, Meaning, and History;* Harrison's *Surnames of the United Kingdom;* and MacLysaght's *Surnames of Ireland.* The list of names was provided from the recollections of Euclid Voyles, Vernedith Voyles (née Payne), and Dorothy Walker Jones. The names in Table 1 represent the people who compose their community.

Table 1
Sandy Gap Surnames

Scottish/Irish/Welsh/German	English	French
Johnson	Stiles	Chastain
McNabb	Beavers	
Craig	Rich	
Walker	Burls	
Runian	Payne	
Roberts	Gladson	
Campbell		
Barton		
Forster		
Flowers		
Fair		
Taylor		
Curley		
Greene		
Graham		
Headrick		
McClure		
Ledford		
Rogers		
Evans		
Voyles		
Clontz		
Elster		
Slagle		

Table 1 shows that 77 percent of the names of residents in the Sandy Gap community are of Celtic, including Germanic, descent. Since intermarriage has taken place between the families, it is likely that everyone connected to Sandy Gap can claim a Celtic heritage.

In recognition of a growing interest in regional development in the United States, it is important to help people understand and appreciate the formation and function of the culture found in the Upland South. The goal of the next few chapters is to help us better understand the Celts and how others see them. In the last chapters we come to appreciate their speech, beliefs, and other folkways.

Through the Eyes of Others

~~~~~~

The first three chapters provide compelling historical evidence and population figures to show that the Upland South is not the home of a dominant Anglo-Saxon people. Instead, the South, including the coastal areas with their large African-American population, is the home of more than 30 million Celtic people. With the exception of the Mississippi Delta and the largely Hispanic Rio Grande Valley area of Texas, the Upland South is the poorest region east of the Rockies.

However, today it may be more accurate to say that there are pockets of poverty as well as areas of wealth scattered throughout the Upland South. In many instances, the wealth in communities such as Metro Atlanta, Nashville, Lexington, and central North Carolina does not directly benefit local people. Rather, much of the economic growth is the result of an influx of non-Southerners and their efforts to diversify industry. Rural communities surrounding those large cities are in danger of losing their Celtic flavor because of urban sprawl.

The expansion of cities into rural areas and the myriad of changes this expansion creates is a serious threat to the South's ancient heritage. As this chapter shows, the rural

South and its folk have been viewed with such negative bias that few non-Southerners regard these changes as a threat to the Celtic culture.

False Anglo-Saxons

Government officials and funding agencies have focused much of their attention on economic problems in the Upland South. In doing so, they have failed to recognize the true heritage of the people and perhaps their most cherished quality—independence. Some scholars and government officials have given attention to isolation as a factor in the economic problems of Appalachia and the Ozarks. They seldom consider the Scotch-Irish way of life as being different from the Anglo-Saxon ethnicity that serves as the basic culture of the Northeast.

Southern mountain-and-hill culture has often been called Anglo-Saxon, even pure Anglo-Saxon. A comparison between Southern culture and the culture of the rugged northern highlands in New England fails to show similar ways of life. If the mountains and valleys did form the unique culture found in the Southern highlands, what could account for the sounds of the people's speech, the way they worship, the way they depend on extended family, and the way they entertain themselves? Would not people in the mountainous areas of New England behave like those in eastern Tennessee, eastern Kentucky, or northern Arkansas?

Even those who hail from the region are sometimes responsible for promoting the idea that the people who live in the mountains and hills of the South are Anglo-Saxons, or, more simply, just plain English folk. For example, Southerner Harry Caudill writes in *Night Comes to the Cumberlands: A Biography of a Depressed Area* that Southern mountaineers were unable to develop a stable social environment because of the deficiency in the quality of their ancestors. According to Caudill, the ancestors of the mountaineers were English pickpockets and thieves or honest men who could not pay their debts.

In the work entitled *Dixie's Forgotten People*, by Wayne Flynt, poor white people in the South are Anglo-Saxons. Their poverty, according to Flynt, is not a reflection of their nationality. After all, he reasons, there are those among them who have done well. His conclusion dismisses the fact that economic and social equality did not exist for Europeans in the 18th and 19th centuries. Immigrant communities were composed of people with differing ability levels, socioeconomic backgrounds, and aspirations. Colonial communities in Southern Appalachia were made up of modestly wealthy, poor, and even homeless people.

Others have used the local dialect to attach a label of inferiority to its speakers. Whether by intent or mishap, those who speak Scotch-Irish (Southern Midlands speech) have been viewed as illiterate, dumb, inbred, or simply genetically deficient, because they are English and their language differs from English Yankees in the Northeast. If an observer traces the dialect of the people back to its place of origin, he or she will find that it is not among the Saxons of southern England. The way the people speak, the values they cherish, the manner in which they use the land, and their attachment to place are clues to their Celtic heritage.

Even the Church in the region is subject to Anglo biases. Did English missionaries from Rhode Island plant Baptist churches in the South? Those who answer *yes* perhaps do so to retain the sentimental notion that Americans were once a common English people. In referring to the migration of the Baptist people and their musical culture, Flynt writes that "New England Baptists collected hymns, which were published in books without tunes. . . . As the Baptists followed the western valleys into the southern Piedmont and mountains, they brought their music with them. In isolated hamlets and rural communities of the Southern highlands—especially Virginia, North Carolina, Kentucky, Tennessee, Alabama, and Georgia— this musical idiom still survived in the twentieth century."

What is not clear from Flynt's description of the movement of

Hiwassee Lake, North Carolina

Baptist people and their culture from New England to the Upland South, which has no apparent historic validity, is that the Baptists in the region have relished instrumental music during the 20th century. This idiom does survive, however, in the Church of Christ, where instrumental music is deemed distasteful because it was not part of the first-century Church. Scotch-Irish Presbyterians in Pennsylvania and Kentucky started the Church of Christ movement in the early 19th century, not mythical Anglo-Saxon immigrants from New England.

The English, or the Anglo-Saxons, enjoyed a different kind of music than the Irish and the Scots. In southern England, for example, youngsters learned to play ballads on the piano, but their Scottish and Irish counterparts did not. The English government viewed the Celtic bagpipe and harp as too ethnocentric and placed pressure on the people to stop playing the instruments. The guitar and fiddle were among the least expensive instruments available, so playing them became common in the borderlands and in Northern Ireland. Those instruments became the foundation of bluegrass and country music.

Celtic people enjoy dancing to lively music. McWhiney describes an event that took place in Virginia during the 19th century. The occasion was a Virginia hoedown, and the person recording the goings-on was an Englishman named William H. Russell. The dancers performed an Irish jig to fiddle and banjo music. Russell was not impressed, and wrote that he thought the music was "uncouth."

Ethnic Identity and Development

Just as the rugged terrain of the Germanic highlands and Great Britain's Border Region once helped to shape and preserve ancient ways of life, so have the uplands of Appalachia, although some changes have occurred. Despite thirty years of effort to develop the region by the Appalachian Regional Commission and other nonprofit organizations, many core Appalachian counties are still terribly depressed. In the mid-1990s, a number of counties had unemployment rates as high as 80 percent. Most government attempts to change the economic plight of the poorest people are ineffective, because the policies are aimed at benefiting traditional racial minorities, and there are few of them in the highland areas. Should attention also be given to ethnic minorities such as the Scotch-Irish or the Welsh?

In those counties that have experienced some development, which is usually caused by tourism and recreation businesses, wages are low for local people and the profits belong to absentee owners. The situation is shockingly similar to the conditions that prevailed in Europe during the great coal-mining days of the Industrial Revolution. The situation in Europe led to mass migrations, but to where are the people of Southern Appalachia and the Ozarks to move?

An understanding of the culture, its origins, and how it works is lacking among those interested in the economic problems in the South, the upland areas in particular. A basic false idea about the people who reside there continues to affect them. Many scholars and government officials have assumed

Bald River Falls, near Tellico Plains, Tennessee

that the people living in the rugged, rural country are there by accident. They are seen simply as unlucky Anglo-Saxons. Some efforts are under way that consider the desires of the local people, like Berea College's Appalachian Center, which headquarters a consortium of 33 private colleges and universities. The purpose of the consortium is to provide appropriate and culturally-sensitive educational opportunities in the region.

Clearly there is a need to rethink the ethics of current government efforts in the region. Correctly viewed, the way of life in the Upland South would have to be considered one of many different expressions of a multicultural society. If adequately understood, the culture of the Upland South would probably receive government protection from being treated with negative policies that attempt to move it into the larger Anglo-American society. Policy makers should try refocusing on the independence and other positive attributes of the resident population. As will be shown in the chapter on attitudes toward politics, federal efforts to help people in core Appalachian counties have led to regionally abnormal voting patterns. A self-help approach might provide the basis for sustained economic and social progress while helping the people recognize, recover, and protect their true ethnic identity.

Meet the Highland Celts

During the 1700s, impoverished Celts from the British Isles cascaded into the valleys of Southern Appalachia like a swollen mountain stream after a spring shower. Leading the way were the Scotch-Irish, who migrated from the Scottish Lowlands via Ulster. It must be pointed out that both the Lowland Scots and the northern English may be referred to as highlanders, because the northern part of Great Britain is much more rugged than the southern farming areas of England. Wales is also more hilly and mountainous than most of Southern England, so the British Celts are called highlanders.

A word of caution must be given, however, with regard to people from Scotland. For example, the term *Lowland Scot* is used to identify a person from southern Scotland, whereas *Highland Scot* generally refers to a person from the northern reaches of the nation, including the western isles, where the country is mostly cold and windswept upland. These distinctions are important, because during the 17th century the Lowland Scots were mostly English-speaking Protestants, while the Highland Scots spoke Gaelic and worshiped in Roman Catholic parishes.

Craig Rossie. The name Craig (crag), which is common in the South, is the Gaelic word for "rock." This ridge is in Perthshire, Scotland, and is a feature of the rugged Lowland landscape of Scotland.

To put it simply, the term *highlander* refers to all Celts from the British Isles, including Ireland. *Highland Scot*, however, refers to a person from northern Scotland. It can be really confusing when one considers the fact that a Lowland Scot can also be called a highlander when the discussion is about Britain. In America's backcountry, Celtic settlers preferred to carve a niche for themselves in hilly and mountainous places that required fewer adjustments in their way of life. The term *highlander* is precisely used to identify America's Southern Celts.

Books on the Southern highlanders have focused attention on their trailblazing feats, Indian-fighting prowess, political skills, and their wild Celtic lifestyle. A number of scholars have written about them in regard to conducting genealogical research. Still others have expressed skepticism about the role of their European ethnicity in shaping their lives in America. In most instances, there is little effort to explain the differences and similarities among the Celts.

Documentaries can also present an inaccurate picture of Southern highlanders, including the Irish and Scotch-Irish. The 1997 A&E Television Network production entitled "The Irish in America" is generous in describing how they have made America their home. Although the early presence of the Scotch-Irish in the colonies is shown, discussions about their contemporary culture and whereabouts are avoided. The film does include a Scotch-Irish notable, Andrew Jackson, the 7th president of the United States. It also makes some references to 18th-century Irish Protestants in the backcountry but is not charitable in describing their culture.

The film accurately points out that many among the Protestant Irish adopted the Scotch-Irish label because they did not wish to be oppressed like the Catholic Irish. The majority of the Catholic Irish were demonized or terribly misrepresented by those who saw them as a threat to the job security of low-wage, unskilled workers. The Catholic Irish were viewed with contempt because they were poor and would accept undesirable and physically demanding jobs at lower wages than their American counterparts. As the film progresses toward contemporary life in America, no distinction is made between the two groups of Irish in America.

There is evidence that early immigrants from Ulster, whether Protestant or Catholic, brought with them a love for the island. In 1737, a group of Protestant Ulstermen and a number of Catholic Irishmen formed Boston's Irish Society. Its initial purpose was to promote and celebrate St. Patrick's Day. A benevolence organization called the Friendly Sons of St. Patrick was formed in Pennsylvania to aid the patriotic veterans of Valley Forge. This organization, composed of Protestant Ulstermen and Catholic Irish, raised $103,500. If these Ulster Protestants living in Pennsylvania had viewed themselves more as Scots, they probably would have joined the Thistle Society, which was composed of Scottish immigrants. The fact that these organizations were formed, in part, by

Ulster-Scots supports the existence of one Irish people, as depicted in the A&E film.

The film left this writer with the impression that the Irish and Scotch-Irish are one and the same. Moreover, the organizations formed by Ulstermen in the early history of our country strongly suggest that the initial immigrants from Ulster were ethnically Irish. This position is probably not an accurate representation of the sentiments held by a majority of the Scotch-Irish today. It is certain, however, that most of the early Ulster immigrants felt a longing for the land that they knew, and that land was in Ireland.

When confronted, in America, with the differences between their culture and that of the Gaelic-speaking Irish Catholics, the Ulster immigrants sought to clarify their identities. As a result, many adopted the Scotch-Irish label. It must be kept in mind that these early frontier settlers descended from poor peasant farmers who left the English borderlands during the 17th century. They were not familiar with the proper terms for labeling things Scottish or Irish. They assumed that the proper name for themselves would be the same as that of the whiskey from Scotland, called *Scotch*. As Kennedy writes, "the form Scotch-Irish would have been used in the vernacular, as 'Scotch' was the proper idiom until the 20th century for both language and people."

Though no formal interview has been conducted which asked modern Scotch-Irish their feelings and preferences toward the Scottish and Irish halves of their heritage, census data collected in 1980 and 1990 suggest that most of them identify more strongly with their Scottish heritage. The government census failed to recognize the Scotch-Irish classification in 1980, but it did in 1990. In 1980 there were 10 million Scots and 40 million Irish in the United States. In 1990, at which time the Scotch-Irish option was presented to Americans, the Irish number dropped 4 percent to 38 million. By comparison, the Scottish number dropped 46 percent to 5.4 million. The negative change for both groups was

6 million, with 4.6 million being lost from the Scottish category.

The fact that there was such a large drop in the Scottish category suggests that Americans of Scotch-Irish descent choose Scottish as their ethnic classification when a Scotch-Irish choice is not available. Logic tells us that if the next census does not provide a Scotch-Irish choice, the Scottish category will be much larger. The numbers, however, do not reveal a negative attitude on the part of the Scotch-Irish toward the Irish. It simply suggests awareness among the Scotch-Irish that their biological and ethnic roots extend back to Scotland. After all, they might reckon, their ancestors lived in Ulster for only a few generations.

Although there is a degree of truth in this statement about their pre-Ulster roots, those who immigrated to Ulster from the Scottish Lowlands and the Border Region during the 17th century had an extensive pedigree reaching well beyond the "bonny banks of Loch Lomond." For example, the Scots line in their ancestry returns to the Irish kingdom of Dalriada (County Antrim) in the 5th century A.D.

Comparisons Among the Irish, Scotch-Irish, and the Scots

As was demonstrated in the previous section, a significant number of Scotch-Irish view themselves more as Scots than they do as Irish. Is there a valid reason for this sentiment? What are the differences between the Irish, the Scots, and the Scotch-Irish? Answers to these questions must include an investigation of each group prior to the Ulster Plantation Movement, which began in 1610. Comparisons between the Irish, Scots, and Scotch-Irish must address the issue of whether or not the Ulster-Scots were assimilated into the Irish culture and to what extent they retained Scottish ways. Although no conclusive statements can be made about the assimilation of the entire Scottish population into the Irish culture, general theories can be articulated that apply to a large segment of the population. To develop these theories, it is important to view the respective groups in a historical and geographical context.

In the waning years of Rome's rule of southern Great Britain, people from the northern parts of the island harassed its legions. A major group that threatened the peace in the northern part of Roman Britain was composed of people known as *Dalriadans*. Their home, which was based in south-western Scotland in a region known as Argyll, was established as a colony of the Irish kingdom of Dalriada. The Romans called them the *Scotti*, or *Scots*. The Scots eventually dominated all of northern Great Britain, which, naturally, became known as Scotland. As a result of their dominant position in northern Great Britain, it is reasonable to insist that the descendants of the people of this region include the Irish in their short list of ancestors.

Scottish people had moved "back" to Ulster over several centuries prior to the 17th-century Plantation Movement in northern Ireland. During that time, Ireland had a type of family-based feudal system introduced by the Normans. Their Celtic clan system merged with the Normans' feudal estate structure. In the process, some clans acquired large tracks of land and governed it and the people who inhabited it in a feudal manner. The Gaelic chiefs O'Donnel and O'Neill recruited many Gaels from the Scottish Highlands and islands to serve them as gallowglasses, or mercenaries.

Gallowglass families included members of the MacDonnell, MacSheehy, and MacSweeney clans. Their first appearance in Ireland as gallowglasses was during the 14th century. Bell adds the families of MacCabe, MacCallion, and MacDonald to the list of Highland Scots that immigrated during the pre-Plantation era. The MacDonnell and MacDonald families were branches, or septs, of the Scottish clan Donald, which bore the title *Lord of the Isles*. At times during its history the Clan Donald had ruled in Antrim, the Isle of Man, much of the Hebrides, and various parts of western Scotland.

Because those Scots spoke Gaelic, they bore more resemblance to their Irish cousins than they did to their Lowland Scottish siblings, who spoke Lowland Scots, a dialect that had evolved from Northumbrian English after the Norman Conquest in 1066. In fact, Bell writes that the gallowglasses in the service of "the warring clans of Ulster . . . quickly adapted to and settled in the Ulster Gaelic society." Bell also observes that since the "time of the creation of the Irish Dalriadic kingdom in Scotland, the two regions and their surnames have been closely related through language, alliance, war, marriage, migration, and trade."

Although many gallowglasses became assimilated into the Irish culture, members of other Highland clans, such as the Buchanans and Stewarts, often associated more with Scottish Lowlanders, who held most of the power in Scotland. Unlike many Highland clans, the Buchanans and Stewarts owned land in the Scottish Lowlands, where the prevailing language was English.

Many families affiliated with clans for protection. Those that did were called *septs*. A family could become a sept through either blood connection or oaths of loyalty. Septs made clans larger and more powerful. Many septs also moved to Ulster, including the Hutson, MacCammie, Morris, Gibson, and MacKibben families. The Hutsons (son of Hugh) and MacCammies (son of James) were septs of the Donald and Stewart clans, respectively. The Morrises, Gibsons, and MacKibbens, to name only a few, were septs of the Buchanans. Two members of those clans, George Buchanan and Francis Makemie (MacCammie of the Stuarts of Bute), became instrumental reformers in the Protestant movement in Scotland and in the New World. A number of the descendants of families such as these eventually became part of the Scotch-Irish people.

Although the Scottish immigrants from the Lowlands and the borderlands lived near many gallowglass and Catholic Irish families, they worshiped Christ differently. The Five

Points of Calvinism, which provided the basis for Reformed theology in the British Isles, was a stark contrast to the grace-and-merit-based salvation system of the Roman Catholics. The Calvinist principles of limited atonement and predestination were troubling to the Irish, as they would be to American evangelical groups such as the Methodists and liberal Baptists. Presbyterianism never displaced Roman Catholicism among the Irish, and there is little evidence to suggest that either group tried to evangelize the other.

According to Leyburn, the scarcity of records indicating interfaith marriages is proof that Catholics and Protestants seldom, if ever, married each other. McWhiney, however, argues that marriages between the two groups were common. This, he reasons, was because both groups were of Celtic extraction and that a significant number of both Protestants and Catholics were merely nominal adherents.

As strong as both arguments sound, the best resolution to the debate over the possible assimilation of the Scots through marriage into the Irish culture is settled by two powerful facts: First, there are few official records or estimates of intermarriages, and second, northern Ireland has only recently begun working toward a peaceful resolution to the historical rift between the two groups. If they were worlds apart during most of the 20th century, then, in all probability, they were worlds apart in 1717, when the first major wave of Scotch-Irish immigrants arrived in Pennsylvania. If marriages did occur, they probably did so in small numbers.

As a result of the Ulster sojourn (approximately 1610 to 1717), the Scots developed a new geographic loyalty, economic and political freedoms, and social mobility, which modified their cultural character. Despite these changes, they clung to attitudes and social institutions that were forged, and seldom modified, on the conflict-ridden border between Scotland and England.

The Lowland Scots living in Ireland brought their attitudes and social institutions with them to Ulster. In time they developed an attachment to Ireland's physical environment. Within a few generations, Scotland, as a homeplace, existed only in the stories and songs of a few people. It was easy for them to transfer their affections. Ulster looked similar to the Lowlands, and its landscape enabled them to continue many of their farming methods.

The Scotch-Irish practice of seeking out new homesites in areas with familiar topographic features continued in the American South. For example, Scotch-Irish homesteaders in Southern Appalachia had large families, and as the regional population increased, numerous younger families sought lands to the west. Many settled in the Ozark uplands, while others traveled to Oklahoma, Texas, and the Pacific Northwest. Those who did not head west ventured into the mountainous and hilly areas of Kentucky, Mississippi, Alabama, Georgia, and to the Florida panhandle. The Scotch-Irish settlers were not environmentalists, but they understood that hills in rugged country could support them with their familiar forms of agriculture (livestock and grains), as well as provide them with protection from hostile foes.

The Scots living in Ulster also learned new ways of working and living. The linen industry gave the Ulster-Scots their first real taste of prosperity. By the time of the first great exodus from Ulster, barely 100 years after the inception of the plantations in 1610, the Scotch-Irish who sailed to America were overwhelmingly better fed and clothed than their Ulster ancestors. The community of Ulster Protestants was now stratified in unfamiliar ways. In the feudal system of southern Scotland their social relationships were based on ascribed criteria (factors which they gained through birth). Ulster offered the Scots a chance for achieved, or earned, status. Social stratification occurred because not all of the Ulster-Scots were equally endowed with natural physical and mental abilities, shrewdness, and motivation.

Ulster also provided the Scots with a political and social environment in which freedom of physical movement and social mobility could become realities. Being released from centuries of living in a feudal system in the Border Region, the Lowland Scots and northern Englishmen were suddenly able to choose to work on a farm or in the city, or to migrate to America. Freedom of choice enabled some Ulster-Scots to rise faster socially and go geographically farther than others in their community, which also created a new set of stratified social relationships.

With the exception of the Ulster experience, the differences between the Highland Scots and the Scotch-Irish are nearly the same as those that divide Scotland's Highlanders and Lowlanders, assuming that comparisons are being made between those who emigrated to the United States during the 18th century. The majority of those differences are due to politics, religion, geography, and economics. Leyburn tells us that King James I, in the early 17th century, did not want more Roman Catholics in Ireland, so all desiring Protestant Scots were allowed to emigrate there. The English were also extended the same offer; but only a small number, mostly from the north of England and the Border Region, accepted the King's invitation.

James felt that the Irish, who were mostly Catholic, would unite with Scottish Catholics, as they had with the gallowglasses. This union of sorts would create more civil trouble in Ireland, which the English government was endeavoring to pacify. The rationale was that the Scots who remained Catholic after the Protestant Reformation during the 16th century were also likely to speak Gaelic. Their form of the Celtic language belongs to the Goidolic language group. Irish Gaelic is also a Goidolic language. Both groups of Catholics, then, would have little trouble finding common interests and would have no difficulty communicating.

Like the gallowglass Scots, the Gaelic-speaking Catholic Scots lived in the Highland region and on islands off the coast. They sought little contact with the Anglicized world, and were generally considered to be the least literate of the Scottish population during the Plantation era. In contrast, the Scottish Lowlanders were overwhelmingly Calvinistic, or Reformed,

Presbyterians. Literacy was assured in the Lowlands because the Scottish Kirk (church) provided parish-school opportunities for its members.

The polarization of the Scottish people into Lowland and Highland spheres of power was produced by political developments that began in the wake of James's ascension to the English throne. James VI, Scotland's Stewart king, inherited the English throne from his cousin Elizabeth I. As England's monarch he became James I. James was the first person to call himself the King of Great Britain, which is the name of the island occupied by England, Scotland, and Wales. Because he ruled on both sides of the border, he was able to pacify the people in the Border Region, which had been nearly lawless through seven centuries of conflict, and apply justice to the bandits that terrorized the area.

The Anglicization of the various languages in Great Britain was encouraged so people could read the newly published King James Version of the Bible. Lowland Scots spoke English long before the 17th century; literacy in the region, however, had only recently become a reality as a result of the Kirk's emphasis on the individual's need to read scripture. The Scots, like their English neighbors across the border, spoke a version of the Northumbrian English dialect. This dialect was a modified form of the language of the Angles who immigrated to the region during the 5th and 6th centuries. The Scots in the Highlands and islands did not share in the Kirk's efforts to promote literacy in the English language.

The Highland Scots maintained a much stronger Celtic culture than the Lowlanders. Until the Battle of Culloden in 1746, the clan system was the primary form of local and regional government in the Highlands, whereas in the Lowlands the feudal system lingered into the early 18th century. There were, however, a number of marauding clans (called *riding clans*) on the border, but King James I pacified them early in the 17th century. The riding clan is an example of a Celtic institution remaining in the Scottish Lowlands and northern England despite many centuries of contact with various conquerors, including Norman-dominated England.

Riding clans on the border between England and Scotland included the Robsons, Charltons, Collingwoods, Tailors, Armstrongs, and Bells, among others. Families such as the Dicksons, Bells, and Grahams, as well as the Hodges and Rogers septs, were well represented on both sides of the border. Sometimes small spelling changes in the name would differentiate the Scottish from the English side of the family. For example, in Scotland, members of the Rogers family would often spell their name with the letter *d* (Rodgers). The Dicksons living in England often spelled their name Dixon. Nonetheless, by 1620 the clan system in the Border Region was comparatively weaker than it was in the Highlands.

Given that most of the early settlers in the backcountry of Appalachia were of Lowland Scots and northern English extraction, it is not difficult to understand why the clan system manifested itself in the Southern highlands of North America. The infamous feud between the Hatfields and the McCoys is an example of the retention of that powerful Celtic folkway over vast temporal and physical expanses.

The last major cultural difference between the Highlanders and Lowlanders to be discussed in this section involves attire. Tartans, kilts, and sporrans were Highland cultural features that did not make their way into the Lowlands until recent years. Traveling through the Scottish Lowlands today, one can find Highland attire commercially displayed, even in border towns such as Gretna Green. The presentation of Highland attire by Lowland merchants is mostly for the consumption of tourists. In the Highland region the sentiment toward the tartan and kilt is much stronger.

The British Highlanders Summarized

It is reasonable to state that the Scotch-Irish who immigrated to the American colonies during the 17th century were essentially Lowland Scots who had lived for a time in Ulster.

Ulster landscape

In Ulster they acquired a knack for making a cash income through the linen and wool industries. It gave many of them a taste for freedom and the material items that personal wealth could buy. In Ulster they lived, worked, and worshiped with others who emigrated from the Scottish Lowlands and northern England, so the retention of many of their cultural traits and dispositions was better facilitated. In fact, when they arrived in the New World, they sought ways to bring their familiar institutions with them. Just like their descendants who moved from Virginia to Kentucky and Tennessee, they arrived in their new settlements with others who were like themselves in ancestry and in culture.

Meet the Germans

The presence of ethnic Germans in Appalachia is not a well-known fact to most people in the South. They are there, but, like the Scotch-Irish, they are also viewed as unlucky Anglo-Saxons. Many of their cultural practices have spread throughout Southern Appalachia. For example, sauerkraut is found in many Southern kitchens. A good percentage of Southerners of German descent claim that heritage from ancestors who never lived in Germany. The country we know as Germany did not exist until the end of the Franco-Prussian War in 1871. These folks are not wrong about their heritage, however, because the medieval kingdoms of northern and central Europe were culturally Germanic.

A large portion of this segment of the South's population might be surprised to know that their German ancestors were in fact Amish, Mennonite, and Moravian Christians from places like Switzerland, Moravia, and Holland. Perhaps their most important contribution to Southern culture is their doctrine of believer (adult) baptism and their desire to separate themselves from civil life, an early form of separation of church and state.

These Anabaptists (rebaptizers) abhorred worldliness. That feeling was especially intense among the Amish. Their coy behaviors and dress are today considered to be quaint, but during the 18th century they were not particularly unusual in their dress or mannerisms. Their dissenting religious views were tolerated in Virginia, where the Anglican Church exerted great influence, because they most often settled in the back-country. Despite their dissension with the Anglican Church, the Germans, as well as the Scotch-Irish, were actually valuable to Virginia's coastland settlements. The frontier families and communities provided the settlers in the tidewater region with a buffer zone against unruly Indians.

Members of other German religious groups also migrated to the colonies during the 18th century. They included a number of Lutherans. The Lutherans in North Carolina, however, were mostly assimilated into other religious movements within 100 years of their arrival.

Over time, trade and intermarriage increased among the backcountry English, German, and Scotch-Irish settlers. Through this intermingling the Southern Appalachian culture emerged. Because of similarities in their cultures, the Scotch-Irish and the English readily mixed, but the Germans spoke a different language and held more peaceful attitudes toward others. Unlike their neighbors from the borderlands of Britain, they were not against cultivating peaceful relationships with the Indians.

Europe had presented each group with different social and geographic circumstances that resulted in their cultural uniqueness in the colonies. For example, the Scotch-Irish and border English were more likely to settle on hilltops or ridgetops. Such sites provided them with excellent vantage points for spotting bandits and other enemies, but because these strategic homesites lacked productive soil, deep-plow cultivation was never fully developed there.

In the Germanic homelands, however, there is an abundance of fertile soil. As a consequence, the Germans brought with them an appreciation for valley lands, which could successfully produce crops. The German settlers were also skilled in other areas. Many of the men were proficient with crafts, such as gunsmithing, as well as various building trades. Those skills, in addition to their farming practices, gave them an advantage over their neighbors from the British Isles. Although fewer in number than the Scotch-Irish in the back-country, the Germans were comparatively more prosperous. The differences among the Germans, northern English, and Scotch-Irish were produced in Europe under a separate set of social and geographic circumstances.

We have already examined the Scotch-Irish and northern English homelands, so let us now focus on who the Germans were and what motivated them to leave their continental domains.

Homelands of the Anabaptists

At the time of the Protestant Reformation, which consumed nearly all of the 16th century, Germany did not exist as a state or unified country. In fact, many royal houses governed Germanic peoples, with the Holy Roman Emperor holding the region together in something less than a loose confederacy. Today, those kingdoms would cover a region extending from the Czech Republic in the east to the Netherlands in the west. The Holy Roman Emperor derived his power from the Pope, as well as from the adherents to the Catholic faith who lived in the region.

Among the Catholic clergy in this region of Europe was a devout priest named Martin Luther. At that time Luther was a professor in Wittenberg, a city located on the Elbe River in present-day Germany. Being bright and well-educated, with a belief that the scriptures were the source of God's revelation and authority, he objected to the sale of prayers for the dead (to gain their release from purgatory), known as *indulgences*. The Church had expanded these sales to raise money to pay the excessive costs associated with the construction of St. Peter's Basilica in Rome.

Luther produced a tract containing 95 theses that argued against the sale of indulgences, and nailed it to the church door at Wittenberg to advertise his desire for an academic debate. Instead of stimulating a colleague to argue the issue, the document brought Luther the wrath of the Holy Roman Emperor. In the early years of the Reformation, Anabaptists were spared the vengeful scrutiny of the emperor because he was preoccupied with silencing Luther and his followers.

Less than four years after the Roman Catholic Church excommunicated Luther and issued a warrant for his life, the first modern adult baptism was performed in Zürich, Switzerland, on January 21, 1525. Conrad Grebel performed the baptism of Georg Blaurock in the house of Felix Manz, beginning the current practice of adult, or believer, baptism. Today this practice is prevalent throughout Southern Appalachia. Blaurock was sprinkled in much the same manner as an infant, a method not widely replicated in Appalachia, where most baptisms are performed by total immersion.

From Switzerland, the Anabaptist movement spread to other German-speaking areas, including southwest Germany, Austria, Moravia, along the Danube River, and down the Rhine River to the Netherlands. Educated clergymen initially led congregations, but because of persecution, leadership roles passed into the hands of men from more humble stations. Congregations were often small and autonomous, so opinions varied from one group to another. For example, while one group might have emphasized pacifism, another group would be less enthusiastic about the position. All congregations consistently adhered to one point, however—the doctrine of believer baptism. Initially they were also interested in *eschatology*, the study of end times prophesies.

The Anabaptist movement nearly ended when a group of men under the leadership of Bernt Knipperdollinck, Jan Mathijs, and Jan Beuckelson (also known as John of Leiden) seized control of the city of Münster. John of Leiden and his followers set up a theocracy and ruled the city from 1534-1535. The zealous rulers advocated polygamy and ran off Protestants and Catholics alike.

Their actions were ruthless, but the Bishop of Münster's reaction was even more brutal. After a 16-month siege, all the leaders of the revolt were captured and executed. John of Leiden's remains were kept in a cage and hung from the rafters of a local building to serve as a deterrent to other would-be revolutionaries. The Münster debacle nearly eliminated the Anabaptist movement in Western Europe.

The solid, moderate leadership of Menno Simmons, however, reinvigorated the Anabaptist movement. Simmons was a Dutchman, but his followers, known as *Mennonites*, came from various locations, including Switzerland and Germany. He and his followers did away with the practice of polygamy, which was advocated by John of Leiden. They focused their attention on the doctrines of pacifism, the working of the Holy Ghost in the everyday lives of believers, the infallibility of scripture, and believer baptism. The doctrines of the early Mennonite movement are expressed in the Dordrecht Confession of Faith. The Dordrecht Confession was hammered out, accepted, and written by Mennonites who attended the national assemblies in 1618 and 1619. Early Anabaptist immigrants to the British colonies would have received theological instruction on the Dordrecht document.

The purpose of the Mennonites might have been to live life as pacifists, but their doctrinal statements reveal a powerful, sovereign God who shows himself only through scripture and the workings of the Holy Spirit. A person's ability to interpret scripture was possible only when aided by the Holy Spirit. These ideas, in addition to the Anabaptist emphasis on end-times scenarios, caused the Mennonites to withdraw from political and other secular social situations in which Christ was not the focus. Similar ideas have been found among many Fundamentalist Baptists living in Southern Appalachia today.

The religious wars that plagued the European continent during the years after the Peace of Augsburg in 1555 was as much a struggle between Calvinists and Lutherans as it was between Calvinists and Roman Catholics. The Augsburg Peace

Accord, which was signed by the Holy Roman Emperor and the Germanic royal houses, created two legal forms of the Christian faith in the Germanic kingdoms of northern Europe: Lutheranism and Roman Catholicism. Calvinists, including the Anabaptists, were not protected by the terms established in the 1555 treaty. Their religious practices were seen as socially inferior by both the Holy Roman Emperor and the Lutheran royal houses, who governed much of northern Europe. These conditions led the Anabaptists, including the Mennonites, to make their way to Holland, a nation of relative religious tolerance.

The climate of religious tolerance in the Netherlands attracted the Puritan group later known as the Pilgrims. Prior to their arrival, however, another English group, under the leadership of an Anglican priest named John Smyth, sought liberty for his group of religious dissenters. In the Netherlands, Smyth met Mennonites who influenced him and his theology. He returned to London with his group, and in 1612 they formed the first Baptist congregation in Britain. Baptist congregations were formed in many other places in England.

Impressed with the Baptist movement in Britain, an Englishman named Roger Williams founded a Baptist congregation at Providence, Rhode Island, in 1639. The first Baptists in America were men and women from England, but it is important to recognize that Williams and his followers were in the Northeast. New England and the Northeast never sent large numbers of settlers into Southern Appalachia.

Explanations for the large number of Baptists in the South have received much attention from scholars. For example, Chadwick summarizes the reasons for the appeal of Baptist-style worship in the Southern backcountry. He notes that a man could become a pastor without a seminary education. There were few seminaries in the colonies, so an isolated congregation could find a man who "felt the calling," build a church, and worship God.

Baptist churches were also appealing because a congregation democratically ran its own affairs. Celts in the backcountry also distrusted political authorities. In Britain, the Church was part of the State. In America it was possible for the Church to shed the autocratic influences of the government. In theory, this removed a barrier between the believer and God. These reasons alone, however, do not explain why people in Southern Appalachia who were not Baptists left their denominations for this somewhat radical expression of the Christian faith.

The Arrival of the Germans

Germans were enticed to come to America by representatives of the Pennsylvania colony and by publications sponsored by entrepreneurs. In fact, William Penn (1644-1718) made a number of trips to Germanic areas, including the Netherlands, to compel the peaceful, hardworking Christians to resettle in Pennsylvania. As was the case with their Scotch-Irish counterparts, the German migration to America began as a trickle. By 1717, however, both German and Scotch-Irish settlers were moving in large numbers.

Another entrepreneur in the early 18th century, Colonel William Byrd II, inherited a large tract of land on the North Carolina/Virginia border and quickly sought to recruit settlers from the Germanic peoples of Europe. In Switzerland in 1738 he published *The New Garden of Eden, Virginia*. As the name suggests, Virginia was represented as a new paradise. Despite the dominance of the Anglican Church in Virginia, hundreds of Swiss Calvinists and their families immigrated to Byrd's lands in southern Virginia and northern North Carolina.

Like their northern British-counterparts, the Germans sought farming opportunities. By this time the Anabaptists had split into conservative and moderate camps. Followers of the conservative Swiss Mennonite Jacob Ammann became known as the *Amish*. They became well established around the city of Lancaster and throughout southeastern Pennsylvania. Most Mennonites settled in those parts of Pennsylvania dominated by the Quakers. Others moved to the backcountry and, like the Scotch-Irish, searched for homesites in less populated areas farther south, in the modern states of Maryland, West Virginia, and Virginia.

Germans, Moravians from the region east of Germany, Swiss farmers, and Dutch artisans peacefully settled together on the American frontier. They selected homesites that offered the best farming conditions, and built sturdy barns and smokehouses to contain and process both cattle and hogs. Until the French and Indian War, their peaceful dispositions reduced friction between themselves and the native Indians. That pacifistic position could not be taken in the case of the Scotch-Irish, who often initiated conflict with the natives, as they had learned to do with the militant Irish in Ulster.

The Germans in the backcountry were a prolific people, and it was not unusual for a family to include between five and ten children. As is the case with the modern German Anabaptists in Pennsylvania, their fertility rates caused a housing problem. Because new families had to find unoccupied land to feed growing children, each successive generation pressed white settlement farther into Indian country. The threat of Indian attack softened their staunch adherence to the principles of pacifism. In fact, the Scotch-Irish and the Germans were allowed to practice Christianity outside the control of the Anglican Church in Virginia only because they provided a frontier buffer against hostile Indians who were allied with the French. Still, families built homes in valleys and hollows that offered fertile, tillable soil but provided little strategic advantage in the event of an attack.

Indian attacks were a serious concern, especially during and after the French and Indian War. Even after the expulsion of the French from the Valley of Virginia in 1763, the Shawnee continued to harass settlements on Kerr's Creek. They annihilated an entire settlement on the Greenbrier River. Another former ally of the French, Chief Pontiac of the Ottawas, renewed attacks on white settlers. In other instances, Mennonite families fled in the face of Indian trouble.

Rouse tells of a group of four Germans who wrote to others in Europe to inform them of their plight in the colonies. He relates that a settlement numbering 39 Mennonite families suffered an attack in which one family was mutilated. The remaining families left everything they owned and fled for their lives. The four frightened Mennonites also stated that during the previous May, Indians killed approximately 50 people, and 200 others were driven away.

For those Germans remaining in the backcountry, social ties grew closer to their more numerous Scotch-Irish neighbors, who never hesitated to fight the Indians, whether justified or not. Nonetheless, the location of German homesites and fertilizing techniques enabled them to gain an economic advantage over the Scotch-Irish, who often settled on the comparatively unproductive summits of hills and ridgetops (thus the nickname *ridge runner*). The Germans were adept at using local limestone and other native rocks to build homes and storage structures. They were also excellent butchers, shoemakers, gunsmiths, mechanics, blacksmiths, papermakers, and ironworkers. The Germans soon supplied items they purchased from Scottish and English importers to their Scotch-Irish and English neighbors. The Germans assumed the highest levels of the rural, backcountry social ladder as a result of their better farming techniques, use of more arable soil, and masterful craftsmanship.

With respect to religion, the Scotch-Irish Presbyterians had difficulty attracting clergy to the frontier, although there were notable exceptions (i.e. the reverends Samuel Doak and Samuel Carrick, who preached Presbyterianism in the South). John Campbell informs us that there are documented instances of Christ-seeking Scotch-Irish families attending Baptist-style worship services. In fact, the very number of Southerners today who claim membership in one of the region's many Baptist denominations indicates that Baptist-style worship won over many Scotch-Irish Presbyterians.

In addition, there is little doubt that many lads and lassies married German youngsters. From an examination of the histories of some families with ties to Southern Appalachia, it is not uncommon to find unions between Germanic settlers and British Celts. For example, the Civil War records of Samuel Collins of East Tennessee states that his grandmother was German and his grandfather was Irish. Pete Randles, who was born in Sevier County, Tennessee, in the middle of the 19th century, was of Swiss, Scotch-Irish, and English descent.

Intermarriage and intermingling caused a union of Celtic British and Germanic cultures in the backcountry, a region that offered little contact with other groups. As a result of assimilation, religious doctrines became mixed, foods became Appalachian, and the sense that the government and all outsiders were to be viewed suspiciously became more intense.

As German families moved south and west from Pennsylvania, many towns and cities were named for Old World places or significant German people. Table 2 shows a brief list of the place-names (toponyms) across the South that have Germanic origins.

Table 2
Germanic Toponyms in the South

Bessemer, Alabama	Hamburg, Mississippi
Coden, Alabama	Heidelberg, Mississippi
DeKalb County, Alabama	Pendorff, Mississippi
Vredenburgh, Alabama	Mecklenburg County, North Carolina
Augsburg, Arkansas	New Bern, North Carolina
Stuttgart, Arkansas	New Hanover County, North Carolina
Berlin, Georgia	Hanover, Pennsylvania
Meigs, Georgia	Germantown, Pennsylvania
Rhine (Rhein), Georgia	DeKalb County, Tennessee
Buechel, Kentucky	Dresden, Tennessee
Erlanger, Kentucky	Germantown, Tennessee
Hessmer, Louisiana	Hohenwald, Tennessee
Krotz Springs, Louisiana	Wartburg, Tennessee
Sondheimer, Louisiana	Meigs County, Tennessee
Bladensburg, Maryland	Newbraunfels, Texas
Dundalk, Maryland	Vienna, Virginia
Gluckstadt, Mississippi	Vienna, West Virginia

Table 2 provides only a portion of the names of cities, towns, and counties scattered across the South that are of Germanic origin. The suffixes of most of those names reveal meanings that are lost in the Southern and Midlands dialects spoken in the region. The ancient suffix *fels*, which means *hills*, is traceable to the tongue shared by both Germanic and Scandinavian groups. The suffix *berg* means mountain, *burg* and *stadt* designate cities, and *dorf* identifies a village.

Despite the many Germanic toponyms on the Southern landscape, the language of the Germanic descendants was obscured by the Northumbrian dialect spoken by the much larger Scotch-Irish population. The next chapter discusses where the unique language of the region originated and how it developed.

Speech Ways Reflect Cultural Development

Because Southern highlanders have an accent that is clearly different from the modern natives of northern Britain and Ulster, it is easy to dismiss the similarities in their respective vocabularies and sentence structures. Admittedly, there are different words used to identify common objects. In Great Britain an elevator is called a *lift*, and cigarettes are called *fags*. A simple comment about smoking on the streets of London, if overheard by an American, could be misunderstood. Nonetheless, the dialect of the Upland South is remarkably similar to the speech ways found in northern Britain during the 18th century.

To fully appreciate the Scotch-Irish dialect (also called Northumbrian and Southern Midlands), it is important to reflect over the parent groups that contributed to its formation. Although isolation from other ethnic groups in America preserved much of its 17th-century vocabulary, conquest, prejudice, and intermarriage with foreigners affected its development. This chapter shows its formation in Northumbria, an area that closely matches the borderlands of Scotland and England.

Dynamics and Levels of Language Development

The Scotch-Irish dialect is unique among language forms, but it is also only one of many variations of English. How does English relate to other European languages? What is meant by the words *dialect* and *accent*? Keep in mind that languages, and culture in general, become different from their parent cultures through social isolation, technological innovation, and social interaction with non-parent-culture members. It may be helpful to remember them as the three *I*'s of cultural and social change.

If we examine the root words found in a language, we will discover words shared with other languages. In the case of common words, we assume that those languages share a common cultural ancestor. For example, in England and on the Isle of Man, one encounters the word *fell*. Sometimes *fel* appears as a suffix, as it does in *Snaefel*, the highest point on the Isle of Man. *Fell*, which means "hill," was borrowed from Old Norse, the language of the Vikings. If we examine enough languages, which many scholars have done, it is possible to place them into distinct language families, which indicates those languages are traceable to a common cultural group. To put linguistic patterns into perspective, you might note that today there are 18 language families around the world that have at least 5 million speakers.

All but four European languages belong to the Indo-European language family. Even American English and Mexican Spanish belong to the Indo-European language family. Language families can be divided into language branches, and Indo-European is no exception. In fact, there are nine different language branches in the Indo-European family. They include Albanian, Armenian, Balto-Slavic, Celtic, Germanic, Greek, Indian, Iranian, and Romance.

Language branches can be divided into groups. For example, the Celtic language branch has two groups, called Goidelic (Gaelic) and Brythonic. North and West Germanic compose the Germanic language branch.

Groups can be broken down into languages. In the case of the Celtic languages, there are Irish, Scots, and Manx Gaelic in the Goidelic group. Breton (spoken in France's Brittany region), Welsh, and Cornish represent the languages in the Brythonic group. English is classified by linguists as a West Germanic language, because it shares more words with the Frisian, German, and Dutch (Netherlandish) languages than it does with the Northern Germanic languages (Danish, Faeroese, Icelandic, Norwegian, and Swedish).

English, despite its classification as a West Germanic language, has many cultural ancestors outside that group, making it difficult to place into any category. The English language is like a cultural magnet. It borrows words from any other language that offers a new idea or object. For example, English has over 10,000 words from French. According to McNeil, some scholars have jokingly said that English should be called a dialect of French.

The standard dialect of English was adopted from the West-Saxon region of southern England. The Saxons came from an area in northwestern Europe that lies on both sides of the Elbe River. Today this area is in northern Germany. Within 100 miles of the Saxon hearth, one finds the Netherlands and the lands of the former Kingdom of Frisia. It is easy, then, to see why the standard dialect of English is considered West Germanic.

Languages can be broken down into local varieties, called *dialects*. Dialects are variations of a language that contain different vocabulary, grammar, and pronunciation than that of the parent language. Understanding can be made more difficult, however, when there is a difference in accent and dialect. The term *accent* refers to the way words sound when pronounced by people with different dialects.

Development of the Scotch-Irish Dialect of English

To a point, as will become obvious, the development of the Scotch-Irish dialect parallels all English dialects, even the Cockney and British Received Pronunciation varieties. In this section we will begin our exploration of the development of those dialects by paying particular attention to the unique aspects of the Northumbrian.

Celts, Romans, Scandinavians, and Germans

The Scotch-Irish originated in the Scottish Lowlands and the Border Region of England. That area of Great Britain was once the homeland of the Northumbrian Kingdom established by Angles from Scandinavia during the Germanic invasions of the 5th century A.D. The Angles' domination of the Celtic people was so complete that only 13 Celtic language words made it into the dialect of English that is spoken there today.

The true British people were Celts. Their arrival in Great Britain dates back to about 2000 B.C. They spoke a Brythonic language. Among their legendary figures is King Arthur, who was probably a former Romanized (Latinized) military officer.

The Britons in the south of what would later be called England were, for the most part, assimilated into the culture of the Romans. The Romans first ventured into Britain during the reign of Julius Caesar, around 54 B.C., and were there to exploit both human and natural resources. They found the climate and terrain of southern Britain to be well suited for cultivation. There were also navigable rivers and excellent harbors in the south. As a consequence, the Romans focused their attention on the resources of that region. In hilly areas with mineral springs, the Romans built baths as resorts for their soldiers.

The Celts were enslaved, and they became the labor force on which the Romans built their infrastructure. To get resources to Rome, the Empire built a network of roads that connected its island holdings to London. The city of London was built by Roman engineers, and it served as their capital in Britain (then known as *Britannia*). Ships loaded with resources from the island set sail for Rome from London's newly constructed docks.

The Romans recruited Celts into their military ranks through coercion and voluntary service because the Italian population had too few males to form a large army. After all, the Roman Empire stretched over a vast expanse of land that extended from Scotland to Palestine and on across North Africa. Most of the soldiers who served in the British legions, especially in the north country, were Romanized Celts.

As the Romans advanced into northern Britain, they found increasing resistance from the Celtic inhabitants. The Brigantes, followers of the Celtic goddess Brigid, and the Picts were persistent adversaries of the Roman legions. In response, Emperor Hadrian ordered the construction of a wall across the

Corbridge Roman ruins, Northumbria, England. This site is about three miles from Hadrian's Wall. The Romans built the wall and this fort to keep Celts out of their realm.

isthmus of northern Great Britain to keep the barbarous Picts out of his realm. In the north, but south of Hadrian's Wall, the Romans built forts to garrison troops to be the vanguard against Celtic excursions into the south.

The groundwork for the differences between the South's Celtic heritage and the Yankee culture of North America was laid by the Romans. You may recall from the first chapter that the Yankee culture was transplanted to America from the southern part of Great Britain. The South's Celtic culture, however, was brought to America by the inhabitants of the rural north of Great Britain and Ireland. As the Roman Empire approached its demise in the West, including Britain, hordes of Saxons invaded the southern part of the island, while Angles and Jutes from Juteland advanced on areas to the north and southeast of London.

Southern Great Britain was the land of plenty for the Romans. The rural north of modern-day England served simply as a buffer zone against the barbarous inhabitants of the cold reaches of Caledonia (a Roman name for the land that would become Scotland). Whereas the northern lands featured garrisons for troops, southern Great Britain gained villas (small towns), roads, established and effective farm practices, a literary tradition, and social class distinctions that saw the Celtic clan system as backward and inferior. The Romans thought Ireland was too cold to colonize, and its inhabitants were regarded as savage people.

During the waning days of imperial Rome, the Church did convert Ireland's pagan Celts to Christianity. That work was accomplish through the tireless efforts of Patrick (c.389-c.461), an early missionary. Once established, the Celtic Church of Ireland sent missionaries, with Columba (521-597) being the first among them, to Caledonia. The Irish and Scots borrowed Greek and Latin words like *altar*, *martyr*, *psalm*, and *angel* and set about to convert the pagan Angles who settled in the north of England and the eastern half of the Scottish Lowlands. Despite the fact that the Celtic Church

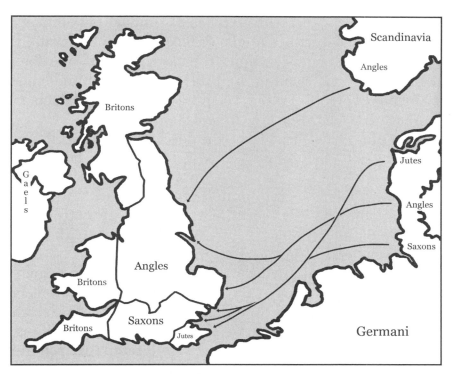

Germanic Migrations into Great Britain, A.D. 400-600

introduced them to Christianity, the Angles never held the Celtic people in high social esteem.

At the time of the Saxon invasions, which began around A.D. 450, the southern Celts, or Britons, like King Arthur, were mostly Romanized Christians. The Saxons abhorred the Celts, and either killed or enslaved the men and women, though some women were taken as brides. Many Celtic men, fearing for themselves and their womenfolk, fled with their families.

From southern England they fled to the mountains of Cymru, or as the Saxons called it, Wales (foreign). Others fled to the rugged land in Cornwall. Celts in the present Midlands area also fled into the rugged but safe Welsh backcountry. The Celts in the north of present-day England scrambled away from the Angles. Much like their southern counterparts, they sought refuge in the hilly and rugged lands to the west. Others went into the Scottish Highlands.

Unfortunately, there are no reliable estimates of how many Celts remained in either Angle- or Saxon-controlled Britain. The Saxons ultimately occupied the more productive regions of Roman Britain. Their imprint on the British cultural landscape has been observed in the modern English dialects of southern and southwestern Great Britain.

The Jutes had little effect on the development of Northumbrian English. Their impact on the British cultural landscape was primarily felt in the areas lying southeast of London. Today the dialect spoken in that region, called *Kentish*, is partly attributable to them. The Angles lived away from the high population centers of southern England, where the Saxons had made their greatest imprint on culture.

The Angles who settled Northumbria provided the linguistic foundation for the Northumbrian dialect. Northumbria extended from just north of the Midlands to southeastern Scotland, including Edinburgh. The Scottish Celts, or Britons, who refused to submit to the Angles migrated into remote regions of Scotland or to the rugged lake country of northwest England. These Celts became part of the kingdom of Strathclyde, which extended from northwestern England through southwestern Scotland. In the Border Region some intermingling occurred between the Scandinavian groups, including the Angles, and the Celtic groups. After a number of years, their ways of life became very similar to one another because of interaction and intermarriage.

Fischer reminds us that by 1600 the inhabitants on both sides of the England/Scotland border were culturally the same people in all aspects except political nationality. Rubenstein insists the Northumbrian dialect in southwestern Scotland emerged as a slightly different version of English after the Norman Conquest of 1066. He refers to this dialect as *Lowland Scottish*. The similarity in both dialects after the Norman pacification of Britain suggests that interaction between the Border English and Scottish was common. Political nationality was the lone factor separating the Scots and the northern English. It was eliminated in Ulster and in Appalachia, where their ethnic identities became Irish and eventually Scotch-Irish.

The Scotch-Irish immigrants in Appalachia possessed both Celtic and Scandinavian cultural traits. During the 9th, 10th, and 11th centuries, Norsemen (Norwegians and Danes) settled the Border Region. The Danes, like the Angles, were from Scandinavia. Unlike the Angles, however, they were also called Vikings and Norsemen. The Viking arrival in Britain occurred in A.D. 793 with the sacking of the Celtic Abbey known as Lindisfarne on Holy Island, which is located just off the coast of Northumbria. At the time of the Viking conquest of Great Britain, the well-established Angles had little trouble com-

Holy Island and Lindisfarne. In A.D. 635, at the request of King Oswald of Northumbria, the Celtic Church in Iona sent Aidan (later St. Aidan) to establish a toehold for Christianity in northern England. The first Viking raid on England occurred here in 793.

municating with their Danish conquerors. Even after 300 years in Great Britain, the language of the Angles, or Anglish (English), was similar to the Scandinavian tongue Old Norse.

Despite the name *English* being ascribed to the language of the British, it was the West Saxon dialect of southern England that had, by the 9th century, emerged as the English standard. The geographic factors that facilitated the Roman domination of the culture of Britain also aided the Saxons. M'Kerlie argues that the Saxon influence was not great in the north of England and in the Scottish Lowlands. At this point, we can be confident that the contributors to the Northumbrian dialect are limited to the various Celtic and Scandinavian peoples who have occupied the troubled region.

The Angles are considered to be Scandinavian because of the location of their continental home. M'Kerlie states, "that the Angles were a Scandinavian people is vouched for by Bede and King Alfred, and their continental home was probably in Slesvig and those islands nearby mentioned by the Norwegian Ottar to King Alfred and by him regarded as the home of the English (Engle) before they came to this country."

Normans

On the west coast of France there is a region known as Normandy. The area was named after the Northmen (Vikings) who settled there, as they had in Britain. In France, King Charles the Simple gave them titles. King Charles was a shrewd ruler who found a willing but demanding ally in Ganger Rolf, the Vikings' chieftain. In 912, Charles gave Ganger the title of Duke and granted him the region known then as Nuestria. The French called the Viking territory *Normandy* (land of the Northmen). The king required the Normans to protect French lands from invaders, including other Vikings. The Northmen were also required to convert to Christianity.

The former Vikings became quite impressed with French culture, but they still possessed their passion for conquest. This passion was evident when they invaded England in 1066.

Instead of traditional Viking beer, they brought barrels of French wine to consume during their conquest of Britain. They also brought a strict moral code and cultural practices that were oriented toward France and southern Europe. In the wake of the Norman Conquest of 1066, England's foreign policies were no longer centered on Denmark and Norway. Instead, France held the interest of the dominant Normans.

During the 12th century, the Normans, acting on an invitation from King David I of Scotland, brought the feudal system into the Scottish Lowlands. The feudal system was essentially a method of land ownership and political rule. Peasants were considered lifetime residents who would cultivate land for their laird (lord) in exchange for protection. The Normans in the Scottish Lowlands were not as numerous as their French-speaking counterparts in southern England. While the Normans in southern England and the Midlands were able to force their ways onto the official culture, namely the government and the Church, their inferior numbers in northern England and in Scotland weakened their ability to dominate culture.

Feudalism did become the way of life in the Border Region, but it soon resembled the Celtic clan system. McDonald informs us that the Norman lords became assimilated into the Celtic way of life. Many of the Scottish clans of note are of Norman origin. As Normans married Anglo-Celtic women, their family names changed. For example, notable Scottish names such as the Weirs of Kelso and the Weirs of Lesmahagow were originally called *De Ver* in Norman French. Robert de Graham, also a Norman, was the first Graham of the famous border clan. The Chisholm clan was also of Norman origin. Their name was spelled *De Chesholm*. In 1124, the Lordship of Annandale was given to the Norman Robert de Bruis, the first of the line that produced Robert the Bruce, the Scottish champion of independence who defeated Edward II at the Battle of Bannockburn in 1314.

Nonetheless, the Norman Conquest spurred the develop-

The River Earn. This tranquil scene in the Lowlands has witnessed numerous battles over the centuries, including the Battle of Dupplin Moor (1332), in which over 3,000 soldiers died in a feud between Scottish families over the throne. North Carolina has a connection to this site. Dupplin County, North Carolina, is the home of many descendents of Scottish immigrants.

ment of the Southern and Midlands English language, as it did the areas of art and architecture. The Northern dialects were not impacted at the same level. The British government conducted its affairs in French for nearly 300 years after the Norman Conquest. The Normans forced the language upon the people of Great Britain and were especially cruel when they did this in the Midlands.

Speaking French became a status symbol for the nobility and the landed gentry. Most of the nobles and gentry in all parts of Great Britain were Normans or their descendants. Though the peasants never completely embraced the French language, their lords and government officials introduced 10,000 words into the Southern and Midland English dialects. The words have never left the English language. It is not uncommon to hear or read these French words in America: boulevard, cuisine, déjà vu, façade, and souvenir.

In 1362, the English government passed the Statute of Pleading Act, making English the official language of England. Today, the official dialect of the United Kingdom is called British Received Pronunciation and is the dialect of the universities and the upper class.

While those cultural developments were occurring in southern England, the basic culture and dialect of the Scotch-Irish was being forged in the north. At the time of the Plantation Movement, which began in 1610 and became a major policy initiative for King James, the north remained culturally in the Middle Ages. It is important to appreciate the economically depressed conditions that existed in the north, because the amenities of culture, including the arts and use of a formal and standardized language, are only affordable to societies that have a surplus of wealth and leisure time.

The presence of large cities in a region is an indication that the workforce is diversified and that there is a surplus of wealth. For example, by 1640 London harbored some 350,000 people, while England's second largest city, Norwich, had a mere 20,000. Other cities and towns were little more than villages. Their lanes and streets quickly changed into paths across the glens and dales of open country. Scotland, Wales, and Ireland were even less developed.

Most villages in Scotland were located within 10 miles of the coast, so the interior of the nation was thinly settled. There were no craft guilds to provide an industrial economic base. As a result, the people in northern England and the Scottish Lowlands had little wealth for the development or purchase of educational experiences. Change in the culture of Northern England and Scotland was slow, if any occurred at all. Leyburn tells us that Scotland was so impoverished at the time of the Plantation Movement that even the lords lacked cash. They possessed only land. When the Plantation Movement began, the Scottish and English peasants living near the border were among the poorest and most culturally backward people in Europe.

As discussed earlier, some Celts were able to read the Holy Bible. Few secular literary works were available, so they had a restricted vocabulary. Because the society had an oral culture, however, great emphasis was placed on nonverbal communication methods such as hand gestures, facial expressions, and posturing. Nonverbal communication remains an important characteristic in the Scotch-Irish culture of Appalachia, as it does in other Celtic cultures.

Scotch-Irish Speech

Many of the words and expressions used by people in the Upland South represent a distinct dialect called *Scotch-Irish*, or *Southern Midlands* speech. Fischer states, "Scholars generally agree that this language developed from the northern, or Northumbrian, English that was spoken in the Lowlands of Scotland, in the North of Ireland, and in the border counties of England during the 17th and early 18th centuries." Because of the presence of isolated communities in Southern Appalachia, many of the Northern-British speech ways are still heard throughout the South.

The dialect has changed, however. For example, settlers in the New World did not have words for things such as squash, canoe, moccasin, moose, chipmunk, or raccoon, so they borrowed those names from the indigenous Americans. Still, the basic language structure and content derives from the Northumbrian dialect.

As the early pioneers settled across the Upland South, they left their mark on the landscape by naming counties and towns after their people or the places where they had lived. The following place names bear witness to their presence and the resilience of their language: Dickson City, Edinboro, and Tyrone, Pennsylvania; Sterling, Stuarts Draft, and Mclean, Virginia; Rogersville, Johnson City, and Knoxville, Tennessee; and Graham, McDowell, and Scotland Counties, North Carolina. Mississippi has its own Caledonia, Skene, and Inverness. There are many more place names across the South that reveal the presence of large numbers of Scotch-Irish settlers. Place names, however, are not the only Scotch-Irish contributions to the language of the Upland South.

The Southern Midlands dialect of the Scotch-Irish in the Upland South is world famous when set to music and folk stories. Southern artists in country music have made great use of their culture's words and themes about love, desertion, God and country, attachment to place and family, and having a great time. Their speech is, according to Fischer, the dialect of "trans-continental truck drivers, cinematic cowboys, and backcountry politicians." It is spoken in the homes and workplaces of the majority of people living in Southern Appalachia and the Ozark Mountains, the Lower Mississippi Valley, Texas, and the Southern Plains.

As Verna Mae Sloane tells in her autobiography, the Southern Midlands dialect has been the source of shame for a number of Celtic people from the Upland South. Their speech has served as the oral basis for "redneck" jokes and the foundation for stereotypical labels such as *hillbilly, ridge runner,* and *hick.* Even with these negative labels, Scotch-Irish people in the Southern highlands continue to speak their ancient tongue. Beyond the structure of double negatives, which we will examine, there are a number of words that are unique to the dialect.

On the following page, Table 3 presents a sample of the terms used by Scotch-Irish people today. The use of these terms was confirmed in field studies conducted by the author among residents of various counties throughout the South. The counties were Cherokee County, North Carolina; Anderson, Roane, and Morgan counties in Tennessee; Newton and McDonald counties in Missouri; and Rogers, Delaware, and Ottawa counties in Oklahoma. Dickson and Fischer provide additional information that is useful when making a connection between many of the words listed in Table 3 and those used by early backcountry settlers and their counterparts in Great Britain.

Table 3
Vocabulary of the Scotch-Irish and Standard English Equivalents

Scotch-Irish	Standard English
Fixin' to	Getting ready to go/do
Thar	There
Whar	Where
Eetch	Itch
Hankerin'	Anxious to go/do
Critter	Creature
Haint	Ghost
Skift	Light dusting of snow
Nigh	Near
Scoot	Slide
Winder	Window
Widder	Awidow
Deef	Deaf
Hard	Hired
Fard	Fired
Brainch	Branch
Lowp	Jump as in a gallop
Lettin' on	Pretend
A-goin'	Going
Young-uns	Young ones, children
Sparkin'	Courting
Far	Fire
You'ns	A plural form of you

The words in Table 3 and their Standard English equivalents illustrate there are differences between the Scotch-Irish and Standard English dialects. By examining, for example, the words *skift* and *dusting*, as well as *lettin' on* and *pretend*, it is easy to see these are different words with the same meaning—evidence of a difference in dialect. The words *brainch* and *branch* are the same words, but they are pronounced differently.

Now let us focus on sentence structure. Although double negatives are not always used in the Southern Midlands dialect, they occur frequently enough to warrant attention. Their use provides extra emphasis on a point the speaker is trying to make. Here are some examples: "My young-uns don't have none of them thangs"; "Nah, I don't wont none of that nanner pudd'n"; and "I ain't never seen none of them thangs!"

Fontana Village, North Carolina, 1954

Verbs are also used differently, especially in regard to tenses. Consider these examples: "Why, I ain't never run in to 'im, d'chew?"; "He done finished for the day"; "She done did it"; "They was thar, I seen 'em"; "Was you borned in a barn?"; and "Ever time I'd he-it the graiund Mama would wharp me one." These sentences clearly maintain a consistent form and composition that differentiates them from sentences in Standard English.

Speech Ways Summarized

The words and expressions presented in this chapter are not relics of the past. They form important components in a living, breathing culture that has a heritage extending into the past well beyond the signing of the Declaration of Independence. It has roots that go back to the Roman days in Great Britain, when clergy from the Celtic Church introduced biblical words to the dialect.

Scholars have given too much credit to the Saxons for their role in helping to shape the culture of northern Great Britain.

This chapter has shown that the Saxons were a primary force in developing the culture of southern Britain. In the north, the Saxon dialect gave way to the tongue of the Angles who formed the kingdom of Northumbria, which once extended from the north side of the English Midlands to Edinburgh, Scotland. Though Northumbria was absorbed into England and Scotland, the dialect was preserved well into the 17th century and the reign of King James, who ruled both Scotland and England. King James facilitated the migration of Presbyterians from the Scottish Lowlands and Protestants from northern England to Ulster.

The immigrants carried their dialect with them to Ulster and eventually to Appalachia. In Appalachia, the Ulster Protestants became known as the Scotch-Irish, and their dialect has been labeled Southern Midlands. After centuries of time and thousands of miles of diffusion, the natural beauty of their ancient words and sentences piece together like a grandmother's quilt, reminding us that life and its circumstances have always been, and forever will be, here.

Souchern Celts in American Sociecy

⊚⊚⊚⊚⊚⊚⊚⊚⊚⊚⊚⊚⊚⊚⊚⊚⊚⊚⊚⊚⊚⊚⊚⊚⊚⊚⊚⊚⊚⊚⊚⊚⊚⊚⊚⊚⊚

The South's Celtic people are one of many ethnic groups that make up America's cultural mosaic. Like most ethnic groups in America from the western part of Europe, the Celts have been in North America for centuries. During much of that time the education system in the United States tried to Anglo-Americanize all immigrants. Social isolation caused by the rugged physical features of the Upland South helped to keep that process from destroying its Celtic culture. As the second chapter demonstrates, the loss of ethnic identity, however, is a different matter. Through the efforts of racial minorities, education and social policies in the United States have recently changed. They are now centered on recognizing and celebrating the cultural contributions of different ethnic groups.

The change away from attempts to Anglo-Americanize citizens has created a new interest, and perhaps awakened a need, among many white Americans to affiliate with their European heritages. According to Robertson, the interest in making ethnic discoveries intensified "significantly in the sixties, perhaps because many working-class ethnics believed that the

WASP [White Anglo-Saxon Protestant]-dominated political authorities were giving preferential treatment to blacks over other minorities." As a result of the common goal among diverse racial and ethnic groups to be honestly recognized, there is widespread support for the social concept known as cultural pluralism, or multiculturalism.

Most of the concerns and issues of the politically active cultural pluralists are addressed through Affirmative Action programs, which seek equal opportunities for underrepresented groups. It does little, however, to reacquaint white people with their non-Anglo ethnic roots.

Non-Anglo whites are still ignored in textbooks and public education curricula. The absence of discussions in the classroom and essays in textbooks on the historical and contemporary issues affecting millions of Celtic-Americans demonstrates society's need to rethink the way in which multicultural education treats the American legacy. Is it reasonable to expect to see Welsh, Scottish, Manx, Irish, Cornish, German, French, Anglo-Irish, or Scotch-Irish histories and cultures taught in American public schools and universities? Is there a chance that achievement tests administered in public schools in the United States will measure students' knowledge of the contributions of Celtic, Roman, German, Scandinavian, and French cultures on America's history and linguistic development?

Many cultural pluralists point out that teaching the English language in public schools along with England's role in colonizing North America is more than enough attention to give to white Americans. They claim that teaching Western civilization is clearly overemphasizing European history in the curricula and that more attention should be given to non-Western groups and their cultures.

There are a few non-Roman-Catholic writers who have expressed concerns about the demise of Celtic culture and identity. R. L. Scott, writing in Billy Kennedy's book entitled *The Scots-Irish in the Hills of Tennessee*, argues that the early Ulster-Scots were plainspoken people with simple lifestyles.

He says, "As early American settlers who were the first Euro-peans to move to the frontier, the Ulster/Scots ethnic identity has never been popularly celebrated in either literature or drama." The second chapter of this book shows that, through natural increase, there should be as many as 20 million Scotch-Irish in America. However, in 1990 only 5.6 million of them could correctly identify their ethnic heritage. Is there concern for the possible loss of this group's cultural identity?

In the current political climate of the United States, which is clearly a multinational state, ethnic survival and cultural preservation can occur in the public arena only with those groups who are active on their own behalf.

Ethnic Pride Is Not Racism

It is not uncommon to hear white Americans complain that African-Americans are allowed to have their own television network, a college fund, and other programs that seem to sug-gest racial preferences against whites. It must be recognized that African-Americans compose an ethnic group because of their common experiences and the fact that the majority of their ancestors were originally from the same geographic area in West Africa. While the African-American community has its lower-, middle-, and upper-class members, their families have had the same cultural experiences for the better part of four centuries. It is, perhaps, justifiably difficult for whites to see African-Americans as an ethnic group because society has focused so much attention on their physiological differences (race). The fact that society encourages the celebration of eth-nic diversity over racial distinctions is only recently being tested by white ethnic groups.

The most active white ethnic groups through the 1980s were the Italians, the Poles, and the Catholic Irish. In earlier attempts to join American society, many of the grandparents of these white ethnics Anglicized their names upon entering the United States. Scots and Germans, also in large numbers, Anglicized their names when they arrived during the 1700s and the 1800s. The sacrifice of their European cultural heritage, reflected in their altered names, was a heavy cost to become Americans.

Still, the thought that the United States government would discriminate against them pushed many Irish into action to revitalize their ethnic identity. Although the Irish have failed to achieve preferential status as far as the government is concerned, they have begun a dialogue between themselves and other groups about the presence of non-Anglo Europeans in America. As a result, according to Robertson, "white ethnic groups now perceive their identity as a potential source of pride and strength, and this has lent further impetus to the society's growing acceptance of pluralism as a whole." This movement has affected other descendants of British Celtic peoples in America.

In fact, the Scottish District Families Association (SDFA) was inaugurated at the 1997 Highland Games at Grandfather Mountain, North Carolina. People of Scots descent whose ancestors emigrated from districts in the Lowlands and who did not belong to the traditional clan system in the Scottish Highlands and islands are eligible to join. Virtually all Southern states have private groups who host Scottish Highland games and Celtic festivals.

The Struggle for Ethnic Identity

As the third chapter shows, there are many erroneous ideas about the ethnic histories of the people who call the Upland South their home. Some of the assumptions about the people and the land they occupy have facilitated negative ethnic labels,such as the derogatory terms *redneck*, *hillbilly*, *ridge runner*, and *cracker,* which are frequently used to identify people from the Upland South. Just as African-Americans have to fight the stigmas associated with stereotyped ethnic monikers, white Southerners from the uplands must do the same. There are a number of organizations that endeavor to help the people of Southern Appalachia identify with an accurate cultural label that embraces the distinct, historically significant contributions to society that have been made by members of their community.

Despite these efforts, however, it must be recognized that stereotypes are painful for many in the Upland South. Forrest McDonald gives us a glimpse into the world of the cracker by discussing Verna Mae Sloane's autobiography. *Cracker* is a term that originally applied to the Scotch-Irish but was later generalized to all Southerners of Celtic extraction. Verna

Mae's story, entitled *What My Heart Wants To Tell*, reveals some of the social and psychological handicaps that many Southerners have felt and experienced. Writing about people who are critical of Southerners, she says:

> [They] have taken our pride and our dignity and have disgraced us in the eyes of the outside world. When our children go into cities for work or are drafted into the army, they are forced to deny their heritage, change their way of talking, and pretend to be someone else, or be made to feel ashamed when they really have something to be proud of.

The Celts in the rural South are the subject of countless "redneck jokes." It is interesting to note that in Britain today the southern English element is considered elite, whereas those who live in the more rural north are called *burrbacks*. Although the geographic locations are reversed, the ethnic composition of the stigmatized and elite groups in Britain is very similar to their counterparts in America.

Shedding Ethnic Labels: Two Opposing Views

There are today two conflicting and opposing opinions on why immigrants to America altered their names to make them sound Anglo-American. As an example, consider which of the following names sound more American: Shea Stadium or O'Shea Stadium, and John Black versus Johannes Schwartz? As these examples illustrate, many Celtic people, including Germans, Anglo-Americanized their names. But why?

One argument says that early immigrants were eager to take part in the blessings of America, including the enjoyment of political and economic freedom. The logic behind this argument could sound like this: adopting an Anglo-sounding name was the fastest way to truly become American. This argument does not see the loss of their ethnic identity as a bad thing. Most educated people would want to be like Anglo-Americans, and what's in a name anyway? They can still have their heritage.

The other point of view claims that the immigrants were trying to avoid negative stereotypes that Anglo-Americans easily attached to ethnic-sounding names. It was necessary in their minds to facilitate entry into American society by shedding themselves of the names they were given at birth, names that reflected the histories of their families. This argument sees the immigrant as someone who, in many respects, came to America because of political oppression or starvation back home. It should be recalled that the early Protestant immigrants from Ireland called themselves Irish. It was only when the Gaelic-speaking, Roman Catholic portion of the Irish population began to arrive in the 1840s and 1850s that the majority of the Protestant Irish in industrial cities chose to call themselves Scotch-Irish. They hoped that by adopting this ethnic label they would be more acceptable to the Anglo-American population.

Efforts to Find an Ethnic Identity

East Tennessee State University and Western Carolina University cosponsor an Ulster-American Heritage Symposium every other year. Their published flyer states that the symposium is to "Encourage scholarly study and public awareness of the Scotch-Irish heritage in North America, particularly in Southern Appalachia." East Tennessee State, Emory, Georgia Southern, Virginia Tech, and Western Carolina universities are also among the few public institutions offering courses that embrace the Scotch-Irish heritage. Church-affiliated institutions, especially seminaries that teach Reformed Theory, also offer courses that include a partial history of the Scotch-Irish.

In recent years, efforts to rediscover Ulster-Scots culture have attracted a good deal of support in Northern Ireland, where the Ulster-Scots people make up a majority of the population. These efforts include their kin who have made America (USA and Canada), South Africa, and Australia their homes. The Ulster-Scots Agency, headquartered in Belfast, has a long-term strategy in place to achieve its goals. According to the organization's mission statement, "The aim of the Ulster-Scots Agency is to promote the study, conservation, development and use of Ulster-Scots as a living language; to encourage and develop the full range of its attendant culture; and to promote an understanding of the history of the Ulster-Scots."

One of the goals of the Ulster-Scots Agency is to promote education that includes instruction and research on the culture's linguistic, historic, and cultural matters. In January 2001, the Ulster-Scots Agency, acting as a partner with the University of Ulster, inaugurated the Institute for Ulster-Scots Studies. The Institute's purpose is:

> To explore the experience of the Ulster-Scots diaspora and its significant influence on the history of the modern world—particularly that of North America.
>
> To unify the histories of the peoples of Ulster, Scotland, and America.
>
> To enlighten perspectives of Ulster/Scots-Irish identity within the USA, Canada, Australia, and New Zealand.
>
> To work with international partners in comparative studies of cultural diversity, regionally, nationally, and internationally.
>
> To provide a forum for debate within the diverse heritages of the island of Ireland.
>
> To locate centrally within the island of Ireland and in Scotland the history, heritage, language, and cultural impact of the Ulster Scots people.
>
> To promote an awareness and understanding of local history and heritage among the people of Ulster.

In America, the Scotch-Irish Society of the USA, since its founding in 1890, has supported and renewed its position on ethnic and national ideals. Its position appears to be in unison with the conservative political forces in the American South.

Dr. John S. MacIntosh, who was the organization's first president, wrote the following statement:

> Born and naturalized citizens, we give ourselves anew in this organization to the land for which our fathers and friends gave their blood and lives. We are not a band of aliens, living here perforce and loving the other land across the sea. We belong to this land, and only recall the old that we may better serve the new, which is our own.

The values and attitudes of the core of the Scotch-Irish community can be described as traditionally American, especially when the following statement from the Scotch-Irish Society of the USA is added to the one above:

> The Scotch-Irish, blessed with energy, courage, enterprise, goodness of heart, and devotion to duty, have left an indelible mark upon the communities where they have dwelt, upon the churches where so many have zealously served, and upon the government in all its branches, where they have supported efforts to bring to reality for all the promise of a way of life the nation's founders envisioned.

The statements made by the Scotch-Irish Society appear to confirm the idea that its members have felt compelled to stress the relationship of their community to the United States. There seems to be little in the statements that would suggest an ethnic uniqueness in America. The Scotch-Irish literally embody the values and attitudes that combine to make one a "good American."

The Ulster-based organizations, however, stress the relationship of the people of Ulster-Scots descent, regardless of their present political nationality, to Ulster, Ireland in general, and to Scotland. There seems to be virtually no emphasis placed on state and national allegiance. On the contrary, their position seems to be focused on the culture and history of the

Entrance to the Ulster American Folk Park, Ireland

Ulster-Scots people. Also among the purposes of the Institute of Ulster-Scots Studies is an acknowledgment of the culture's diaspora. The Scotch-Irish Society insists that its community is "not a band of aliens living here perforce" (without choice), when in fact they had little choice but to immigrate to America.

When one examines the aims and purposes of the Ulster- and American-based organizations that are dedicated to the Ulster-Scots people, it becomes clear that a sense of ethnic identity and purpose is not uniformly shared. That diversity is perhaps the result of the diaspora itself and the cultural and political reality of the contemporary Ulster-Scots people, and it is seen in the various ethnic labels that are used today. The label "Scotch-Irish" is an Americanism, and those who have European perspectives may elect to call themselves Scots-Irish or Ulster-Scots. Clearly, there is difficulty in a hyphenated label such as Ulster-Scots-American. It is much simpler to use Ulster-American. Of course there are those who prefer the nationalistic labels of Irish-American, Scottish-American, or, as 12 million in the South prefer, "American only."

Attitudes Toward Politics

@@

As it was in the Celtic lands of Britain, the South does not have a tradition of a strong central government. Looking back through time, it is clear that the conservative nature of the Celtic South was brought here from the Old World. For example, the folks of the Border Region relied on the feudal-clan system of governance. In those days, law and order were the purview of the lord and his ilk. Feuds like the infamous Hatfield and McCoy struggle in Kentucky were the normal way of seeking justice in the Celtic lands of the British Isles.

Just like the feuds in Southern folklore and history that were brought from Scotland, so too was the Upland South's disdain for taxes to support big government. The American South, as compared to the North, does not support taxation. In fact, Tennessee's Democratic governor, Phil Bredesen, won election in 2002 partly on a promise of no state income tax for Tennesseans.

At the peak of Scottish migration to Ulster in the late 1690s, famine was a threat to the survival of many in the Lowlands. In fact, it is estimated that between one-third and one-half of the population either died from starvation or immigrated to

Ulster. One proposal that was put forth at the time involved a temporary poor rate to aid the needy. The English, in a manner similar to attitudes in the United States' North, had accepted the idea. Some justices in the Scottish lowlands threatened to strike if it were enacted. At least one Scot remarked that the proposal was "odious and smellis of ane taxatioun" and that it was "nathair a credeit ner benefeit" to anyone. The poor-rate was not successful in Scotland.

In the Civil War, the South's Celts chose a confederacy as its form of government. A confederacy is a loose union with decentralized power. The South has supported conservative politics for most of its history. In the Upland South, but away from core Appalachian counties like Buchanan County, Virginia, and Floyd County, Kentucky, politicians are most successful if they are Republican Party members and desire stiff penalties for crime, including a favorable stance on capital punishment, and a smaller, less intrusive government. Local politicians tend to avoid environmental issues because extractive industries like tobacco farming, coal mining, and logging are important in the region.

As one might expect from a region known as the Bible Belt, voters in the Upland South tend to favor politicians whose stand on moral issues is conservative. Successful politicians avoid public statements in support of gay rights and government assistance for abortion-on-demand. While gun control is not necessarily a moral issue, the right to bear arms is a popular position to support.

The South has always been conservative, but its preferred party affiliation has changed over the years. During the years that followed the Civil War, the South was a stronghold of the Democratic Party (*Dixiecrats* in the South), although areas of the Upland South were pro-Union during the war and mostly Republican after the conflict. The Dixiecrats favored retention of slavery, while the Grand Old Party (GOP) of Lincoln wanted to abolish slavery. After the Civil War and during Reconstruction, Southerners generally regarded Republicans from the

North as meddling carpetbaggers who wanted to change the South by empowering former slaves.

Since the 1930s, however, African-Americans have increasingly found strong support among Democrats. In the 2000 presidential election, 95 percent of African-American voters cast their ballots for the Democratic ticket. Today, the Republican Party sees its role in society as the guarantor of individual freedoms and tries to avoid promoting programs that differentiate Americans by racial and ethnic groups. This position appeals to white Southerners who have felt that Democrats do not have their best interests at heart, including support of their cultural values, which embody the concept of natural liberty (individual freedom).

The positions of the Republicans have attracted many voters away from the Democratic Party. As Allen Dennis, a former professor of history at Mississippi's Delta State University, said, "It was not the South that left the Democratic Party. It was the Democratic Party that left the South." Mississippi, once a stronghold of the Dixiecrats, had its first two-term Republican governor during the 1990s. Both of its senators are members of Abraham Lincoln's Grand Old Party.

Tennessee has had two geopolitical realms since the Civil War: the Republican East and the Democrat-controlled Middle and West. Today the state has a Republican governor, and like Mississippi, both of its senators are Republicans. It is interesting that this change occurred in Tennessee and the South during the Clinton/Gore administration, despite the fact that former president Bill Clinton hails from Arkansas and Al Gore is from Carthage, Tennessee. The South has witnessed an unprecedented move away from the Democratic party.

Georgia has flirted with becoming a Republican stronghold. From 1995 to 1999, Newt Gingrich, a GOP representative from the northern part of the state, served the nation as Speaker of the House of Representatives. In the presidential election of 2000, George W. Bush won the state with 56 percent of the total votes cast for the two major parties. In the northern highland counties, however, Bush won by a much larger percentage. For example, in Gilmer and Forsyth counties Bush received 69 and 81 percent of the major-party vote, respectively.

The highland counties of Arkansas are also staunch Republican areas. These counties include the historically conservative Third Congressional District, whose seat was held for 26 years by the Republican stalwart John Paul Hammerschmidt. While George W. Bush collected 53 percent of the entire state's major-party vote, Benton and Carroll Counties cast 67 and 61 percent of their major-party votes for the Republican. Boone County, Hammerschmidt's home, gave Bush a 66 percent victory.

Texas was once considered to be squarely in the Democratic fold, but since Republican George W. Bush's 1994 gubernatorial election over the popular, outspoken Democrat Ann Richards, the state has grown more Republican in its support of politicians. Both of its senators are members of the GOP. Like in Tennessee, Kentucky, Georgia, Oklahoma, and Texas, Democratic politicians are considered to be cultural conservatives (anti-abortion, pro school choice) but fiscal liberals (i.e., government programs and spending to help the working man). The South's Celts seem to vote for politicians who do not threaten their perceived natural liberties (i.e., ownership of resources and the right to bear arms).

The 2000 presidential election can be seen as a reflection of rural/urban and North/South divisions and has ethnic implications as well. Despite Al Gore's narrow victory in the popular vote, he lost in the Electoral College. Much attention has been given to how racial minorities voted in the election of 2000. For example, over 90 percent of blacks who voted cast their ballots for the Gore/Lieberman ticket. Typical analyses suggest that urban African-Americans want an activist government that will help them amend economic and social injustices.

There is little doubt this interpretation of the voting patterns is accurate. It does not, however, offer an explanation as to why every Southern state, despite large African-American populations and the fact that Al Gore hails from the South, voted for George W. Bush. Further, 32 states voted for Bush, and only 18 voted for Gore. The South and the Mountain states voted Republican, whereas the metropolitan and organized-labor populations of the Northeast and other regions voted Democratic.

It has been over 135 years since the end of the Civil War, and it would seem the ideas supporting a strong, activist federal government are still felt in the urban North. Conversely, it would seem rural Southerners still desire to live in dominion over nature, to abide by God's moral code, and to let well enough alone.

One of the last Southern states to maintain a large population of conservative white Democrats is Oklahoma. According to Jeff Birdsong, a political scientist at Northeastern Oklahoma A&M College, Democrats remaining loyal to the party label do so simply because it keeps with tradition. He also states that most of Oklahoma's Democrats are cultural conservatives who see the government as an instrument to help the working man. The conservative orientation of the party faithful is due in large measure to the number of Southern Baptist congregations in the state. Although Oklahoma's political history is one that embraces Democratic candidates, the state greeted the 21st century with a Republican governor, a rarity in Oklahoma's history, and two Republican United States Senators.

Oklahoma and the states in the Upland South are not becoming conservative as they increasingly cast their votes for Republican Party candidates. The Celtic South has a tradition of conservative politics. The parties have changed places on conservative issues and their promise of a less intrusive federal government. The loosely linked confederate form of government the South chose during the Civil War epitomized the Celtic disdain for a strong central authority.

Today, the Republican Party offers the freedom-loving Celts less intrusion while reassuring them that their way of life will not be a target for the central government. Voting patterns in the Upland South are not likely to change as long as the parties continue their respective stands on fiscal and moral issues.

Attitudes Toward
Order and Violence

@@@

In the borderlands of Britain during the Plantation Movement, violence was an appropriate response to perceived wrongdoings. Celtic culture, wherever it has been found, has been regarded as violent. McWhiney says, "proud and contentious Scots, Irish, Welsh, and other Celtic people . . . were ever ready for mass combat or individual duel." Dr. Samuel Johnson, an 18th-century chronicler of the Scottish Highlands and its people, described public processions there, whether solemn or festive, as occasions for local lads to do battle. Thomas Crofton Croker, who conducted research in Ireland during the early 1800s, described the Irish people as being "wild and unruly, barbarous, and warlike." In the South, young boys are taught to respect masculine traits and to idolize men who are brave, strong, and able to fight for just causes, and girls are taught to respect those traits.

Differences in violent-crime rates in America's states and regions illustrate the continuation of the Celtic method of solving problems with acts of violence. In 1982, Massachusetts and Minnesota, both of which are racially and ethnically diverse, had rates of 3.8 and 2.3 homicides per 100,000 people, respectively. Texas, on the other hand, boasted a rate of 16.1 homicides per 100,000 people. At the same time, the Southern highland states averaged 14.7 murders per 100,000 people. Kansas and North Dakota had murder rates of 5.7 and .9 per 100,000, respectively. The South's higher numbers are suggestive of a culture prone to use violence to solve problems.

Are higher violent-crime rates in the South a reflection of the Celts' way of exacting justice in the manner that had served their ancestors in their lawless homelands? Interestingly, many scholars have chosen not to consider this explanation to account for the regional differences in violent crimes. Instead, they argue that social and economic inequalities explain the high incidence of violent crime. In this model, poverty causes people to become frustrated due to relative deprivation (a group's affluence as compared to others). Being frustrated, they act violently. If this argument were valid, poor hilltop towns in New England would also experience high homicide rates, but they do not. Other factors must contribute to the violent tendencies inherent in the culture of the South.

Some have argued that ethnic diversity in urban areas results in violent crime. Many Southern highland towns and cities, despite a lack of ethnic diversity, have homicide rates that are higher than their Northern counterparts. Northern cities such as Detroit, Michigan, have ethnically contrastive neighborhoods, including areas heavily settled by Southerners from the uplands. According to Fischer, the greatest frequency of homicides in large urban areas in the North occurs in neighborhoods composed of people from the Southern highlands. Evidently, transplanted Southerners have taken their violent tendencies with them to the urban North. When we exclude economic, racial, and population density as factors contributing to the high incidence of murders, we are left with cultural explanations.

More evidence of a cultural connection to violence comes from Sandy Gap, North Carolina, the mountain community that has previously been discussed. In Sandy Gap, the Johnson, Walker, and Voyles families have experienced Border Celt justice in painful ways.

Vernedith Voyles relates an incident that occurred in 1917:

> They was having a meetin' over at the old Baker house when seventeen-year-old Dolly Voyles was killed. Pastor Black [an alias] was a-preachin', I believe, and Dolly seemed to be in the spirit, when the worshipers heard a commotion outside whar some of the menfolk was talkin'. The Johnsons and the Voyles men was fightin' and gettin' purty loud. Somebody said that a Johnson boy, who was a-scufflin' with Everett Voyles, come round from behind the makeshift church and pleaded with his daddy for help, 'cause he'd been cut. The old man Johnson looked at his boy's wound and said that he'd been hurt worse 'n that in a briar patch.
>
> The folks in the house were getting purty upset, when Dolly stood up with a trancelike look on her face. I reckon she was a-feelin' the spirit. She stood up and looked to the ceiling with her arms open wide and said aloud, "Yer guns and knives won't hurt me."
>
> When she said that, a Baker man stood up and hollered, "Well, we'll see 'bout that." That Baker man reached in his pocket, pulled out a little gun, and aimed it at Dolly. He shot her afore anybody could stop 'im.

The bullet struck Dolly in the stomach, and she died a few days later. No one was arrested. Informal justice was pursued to no avail, because of blood and marital ties between the families. When asked about the Sheriff Department's role in investigating Dolly's murder, Vernedith remarked that she "thought there had been a report filed, but nobody really expected the law to do anything." Many members of the Johnson and Voyles families remained at odds for a number of years after the young girl's murder. It is interesting to note that Vernedith Voyles is the granddaughter of Elizabeth Johnson, and the sister-in-law of Dolly Voyles.

Vernedith Voyles

Alvin Flowers, who was born and raised in Sandy Gap, shared a story about his half brother Frank, who was born in 1925. Frank's mother had four children, but by the time the three youngest were old enough to remember interacting with Frank, he was grown and living on his own, albeit it was in "the next holler over."

Frank was well mannered when he was sober, but he could be a demon when drunk. The same could be said for most of his boyhood friends who remained in the mountain community. One night in 1960, Frank, who had not been drinking, arrived at his mother's home with Mary, his new bride. Frank's teenage cousin Dorothy was there with her older husband, John Walker. John was using profanity in front of the women, so Frank told him to stop. The men exchanged heated words. Finally, Frank accused John of mistreating Dorothy, and a fight followed. Frank's larger size gave him an advantage over John, and he got the best of his cousin-in-law.

A few months later, all the trouble was behind the longtime friends. Some men in the community, including Frank and a man named Leonard Clontz, went over to John Walker's for a Sunday afternoon of whiskey drinking and storytelling. John and Leonard began to argue, and it soon turned into a fight. John was losing the fight, so Frank pulled Leonard away. Out in the yard, Leonard pummeled Frank with a small handgun. Frank used his tremendous size and strength to hurl his opponent around the yard, despite Leonard's initial advantage. Frank let him go, and some of the men urged Leonard to go home and cool off.

Leonard got into his car, and since it was warm weather, he took time to roll down the window. Frank, who had now decided not to let Leonard go home, ran to his scared friend's car, which was slowly backing out of the dirt driveway. When he reached the vehicle, Frank tried to hit Leonard through the open window. Leonard, still shaking with fear and holding his .22-caliber pistol, raised it and aimed at Frank's right temple. With a trembling hand, he fired into Frank's defenseless head, causing him to slump to the ground.

Though the shooting was investigated, Leonard did not serve a prison sentence. Frank did not die from his wounds, but because the bullet had traveled through his brain, he was partially paralyzed. The bullet was never removed. In the wake of the incident, Frank's thirst for alcohol increased, while his desire for human companionship, including his interest in women, waned.

Two years later, in 1962, Frank's body was found with a bullet hole through the chest. Because his rifle lay beside him along with a note stating, "I have never been successful but maybe this will be a success," the Cherokee County Sheriffs Department decided that Frank's death was the result of a self-inflicted gunshot wound. Soon after, Leonard Clontz met up with Frank's best friend, H. Dodson, and a fight over Frank ensued. Dodson beat Leonard severely. Leonard recovered and later stalked and killed Dodson. He served an 18-year prison sentence for the murder.

Leonard's time in prison did little to cause him to avoid trouble. A short while after his release from prison, Leonard visited a friend named Roy Rich. Despite being old friends, a quarrel developed between the two men. Roy pulled out a gun and shot Leonard, ending his life.

* * *

(l. to r.) Frank Voyles and uncles Felix, Jasper, John, Rufus, and Everett Voyles at the Voyles homeplace, Cherokee County, North Carolina

For people coming into the region from other places, especially if they are from the North or between the ages of 8 and 18, life can be difficult. Children in the South are socialized early in life among siblings, cousins, and those with long-standing ties with the family. Not all aggression against non-locals is of a physical nature. Excluding people from social situations (social closure) and public ridicule are often used in lieu of physical assault. Even adults find it difficult, if not impossible, to become accepted in the community. This is less likely to happen in college towns and cities, such as Knoxville, Tennessee, which are magnets to well-educated people from other regions. In places such as these, nonlocal children can find social cliques more numerous and easier to enter. In Southern Upland places that are removed from the cosmopolitan influences of an institute of higher learning or a large technical firm, the effects of social closure on nonlocal children, and even their parents, can be devastating.

Settlements within a geographic region, such as the Cumberland Plateau, which extends through Kentucky and Tennessee, are often isolated from each other because of the rugged topography as well as the clan-like social closure. The same phenomenon occurs in Ireland. In fact, the isolation of one village from another is so strong in Ireland that differences in dialect have developed between them.

Outsiders in Appalachia have often been seen as foreigners, even if they are Americans from nearby mountain communities. Consider the case of Dan, who moved into a Morgan County, Tennessee, community. Although they had roots in the region, life was tough for this young man and his family. Dan's family moved to the community when he was in primary school. Social groups (cliques) in his grade were already formed when he settled into his new classroom. As a result, he found few opportunities for friendship. Most of his attempts to play with other children were rejected. Instead, the children subjected him to physical and verbal abuse. Dan withdrew socially and academically, as he did in almost every other aspect of his life.

The irony of Dan's situation is that his parents had chosen to move to the country because they thought being there would provide them with a natural, loving lifestyle in which there was no need for the stricture of laws to govern social behaviors. Sociologists refer to this way of life as *gemeinschaft*.

In the case of Sandy Gap, the incidents described were not the result of drug or whiskey deals gone sour. They began as domestic disputes and evolved into acts of retribution for perceived wrongdoings. Clearly, in the small North Carolina mountain community, Celtic justice was practiced during the 20th century. Dan's experience in the Morgan County area of Tennessee is evidence of social closure enacted by a Celtic people who learn at an early age to use physical and psychological violence to protect themselves from outsiders. Unfortunately, their methods can be devastating to youngsters who are not part of their group.

These accounts of violence and closed social settings paint

Mountain view in Morgan County, Tennessee

a negative portrait of the Upland South. As negative as it might seem, the incidents are true and deserve an explanation. However, there are mitigating factors that offset violent behaviors. Many people in the Upland South are quite loving and will give of themselves at the first hint that help is needed, whether asked to or not, even if the person needing help is an outsider. What explains this benevolent behavior in a region where violence is so commonplace? It could be that the factors creating this benevolent condition are too complex to identify. As the next chapter shows, however, a basic answer can be found in religion and the pervasive effect it has on many of the Upland South's social institutions.

Chrisτian Rooτs

@@

In this chapter we examine the roots of Southern Christianity. To do so, it is necessary for our quest to begin in Scotland with the events that led to the Scottish Reformation. The Scottish Reformation serves as the basis for the political and religious events that added fuel to the Plantation Movement in Catholic Ulster. It is also important to start at this time in history because it was during these years that perhaps one of the greatest gifts to Southern Christianity was bequeathed. This gift is the King James Version of the Holy Bible.

It is perhaps difficult to imagine that the man who authorized the English translation of the sacred scriptures that is so highly regarded by Protestants would be born into a Roman Catholic family. King James VI of Scotland was born in 1566, the only son of a marriage between Mary, Queen of Scots, and her cousin Henry Stewart, Lord Darnley. At the time of James's birth, the Scottish Reformation was only six years old, and the fires of Protestant revival were burning brightly in southern Scotland. Sadly for the infant, his father was murdered, allegedly by the man whom his mother soon married. Mary's hasty marriage to the Earl of Bothwell in the wake of her husband's violent death was a profoundly inept political move to make in a country bent on attaining pious Christian perfection.

Darnley's death and Mary's subsequent marriage sparked a short-lived civil war that ended her reign and honeymoon. Her disgraced husband fled to Denmark, and Mary sought refuge from her cousin Queen Elizabeth I of England. Being a Protestant, Elizabeth refused to meet with Mary, who, despite her problems at home, was an heir to the English crown. She was arrested and incarcerated. While Mary, Queen of Scots, languished in English prisons until her execution in 1587, Scotland was governed by a regent on behalf of her son. As a youngster, James was taught theology and academic subjects by Calvinist Protestants.

In appearance, James was an ungainly and shambling man. Perhaps because of his Calvinist upbringing, he was deeply interested in theology. He was brilliant, but his intellect was tempered by a wayward and prickly personality. Unlike Queen Elizabeth, he was extremely shy in the public arena. As an administrator, James was generous in his political favors to people, including those of questionable integrity and political talents.

Besides his mother, James was the only living heir to the English throne. With his eyes firmly fixed on his future, he relished the thought of inheriting the power and wealth that came with the uncontested throne of England. Perhaps because his mother was his only competition, he never begged her captor for her life, nor did he ever visit her in prison. James wanted to ensure for himself a smooth ascension to power upon Queen Elizabeth's death, so he continually sought her favor.

James's efforts to please Queen Elizabeth's court did not go unrewarded. In 1603 James VI of Scotland assumed the English monarchy. While still reigning as Scotland's James VI, he moved his residence to London to become England's King James I. Afterward he ventured back to Scotland only once. James was the first monarch to have the power and resources to bring law and order to the Border Region. In recognition of this fact, he gave himself the title of King of Great Britain.

Despite King James's moral shortcomings, he made a pos-

Stirling Castle. This is the childhood home of Scotland's King James VI.

itive impact on the lives of borderland peasants, who had never known freedom and prosperity. To the Protestant and English-speaking people of the Lowlands he granted lands in Ulster. Many Lowland peasants, especially those in the Border Region, must have seen James as a liberating hero similar to the way former slaves regarded President Abraham Lincoln. To the peasant's descendants who made their way into Appalachia's backcountry, James's legacy was unimpeachable. Today, many descendants of the South's pioneering Celts still respect King James and regard his version of the Bible as the final authority on God's revelation to humanity.

Anglican and Presbyterian Church Structures

When Henry VIII officially broke away from the Roman Catholic Church in 1534, he maintained the episcopalian structure of the Roman Catholic Church. There was one major difference, however. The Pope was no longer the head of the English (Anglican) Church. The monarchy assumed the headship and directed all major ecclesiastical policies. In Scotland, the Protestant Reformation arrived in 1560 under the strong leadership of John Knox, a Scot who had studied theology and church organization under John Calvin in Geneva.

Although King James was raised by Calvinists in Scotland, he and his son Charles I and grandson Charles II tried unsuccessfully to impose the episcopal structure on Scotland. They intended to create a uniform church structure with the monarchy as its head. This structure would make it less troublesome to govern the Christian people of England and Scotland.

Theologically, the two church systems became increasingly alike as the Calvinist ideas of the Protestant Reformation swept through England, a result of the work of Puritan reformers. In the years 1643-1647, an Assembly of Divines was convened at Westminster in England. The fruit of their work was the "Westminster Confession of Faith Together with the Larger Catechism and Shorter Catechism with Scripture Proofs." Despite similarities in theology, the two churches maintained different organizational structures.

The episcopal organization of the Anglican Church has a centralized power structure. In such a system the priest or rector answers directly to a bishop, who in turn answers to an archbishop. The Presbyterian form of government is oftentimes mistakenly attributed to John Knox. In fact, he was indifferent to that form of government. Knox's successor, Andrew Melville, who was head of the Kirk from 1574 to 1606, actually laid the groundwork for establishing Presbyterianism as the form of Kirk governance in Scotland.

In a sense, Melville became an early martyr for a Presbyterian Kirk, because King James forced him into exile. Despite his efforts and personal sacrifice, however, Melville's preferred form of church governance would not become a permanent fixture in Scotland until 1690. Interestingly, Presbyterianism was permanently established in Ireland (1642) and America (1683) before its establishment in Scotland, the land that originally begat the idea.

Although the term *presbyterian* refers to this form of church governance, it is easy to misuse the label *Presbyterian* when referring to the theological teachings of Calvin and his followers, including those of Scotland's John Knox. Calvin's theology is called Reformed Faith, so a distinction can be made between a Presbyterian church's theological position and its governmental structure. In a presbyterian church, the congregation elects presbyters, or elders, to manage the congregation's affairs.

Unlike presbyterianism, which is based on a representative democracy, 16th-century Scottish episcopacy was a dictatorship and the king was the one in charge. To fully appreciate limited democracy in the Kirk, it is important to examine the secular and spiritual needs of the Scottish people that led them to revival and reform in church governance.

Scotland's Call for Reformation

The Scottish Reformation was a Calvinist movement that emanated from the people. Prior to the Reformation, Scotland was essentially a Christian nation in the Roman Catholic tradition. Its ecclesiastical body was an abused institution in desperate need of a clear theological mission and efficient and accountable church management. Like a conquering crusader from centuries past, John Knox came home to Scotland. He was not armed with material weapons. In his mind, he had the sword of God at his disposal. Knox carried with him John Calvin's Reformed Theology, and he found the Scottish people ripe for change.

John Calvin, who lived from 1509 to 1564, witnessed Luther's schism with the Roman Catholic Church and the subsequent persecution of Protestants in Calvin's native France. He agreed with Luther's views that scripture is God's revelation of Himself to humanity, that salvation is a free gift of God, and that the Pope's dictates did not represent God's will.

Vocationally, Calvin was a lawyer. His studious mind found great deviation in scriptural writings and the teachings and practices of the Roman Church. For example, Luther and Calvin believed that the Pope had no more ability to interpret God's will than anyone else who could read scripture and be led by faith through the Holy Spirit. Unlike the Roman Catholic Church, Calvin and Luther similarly taught three important theological doctrines that were seen as a departure from Catholicism. The three doctrines pertained to salvation and God's Word and will. The three doctrines are *sola fide* (faith alone), *sola gratia* (grace alone), and *sola scriptura* (scripture alone).

The Roman Catholic Church has steadfastly refuted arguments that it teaches dissimilar doctrines of salvation since the A.D. 418 Council of Carthage, which condemned the heretical teachings of Pelagious, who taught that humans could abide by God's law with no help from the Holy Spirit. According to R. C. Sproul, "Rome has always insisted that faith is a necessary condition of justification [salvation]. What they have denied historically is that it is a sufficient condition. The Reformation was waged, not over the question of justification by faith, but over the issue of justification by faith alone."

Put simply, the Reformers believed that God reveals His will through reading or hearing the inspired words of the Bible, and salvation is given freely by grace to those with faith. Faith is a product of regeneration and is in itself a free gift from God through the Holy Spirit. In the Catholic view, faith is a condition of salvation. Contrary to the teachings of Rome, Luther and Calvin believed that the apostle Paul clearly wrote about the means of salvation, and that the Pope did not have the authority to sell prayers for the dead (indulgences) to free the departed from purgatory. According to Catholicism, those who had not achieved a level of Christlike perfection in their earthly life were sent to purgatory to be purged of their sinful ways. The reformers did not see any scriptural evidence to support the existence of such a place, let alone an authorization for the Church to profit from it.

Calvin, however, departed from Luther in his ideas about

St. Serf's Church and cemetery in Dunning, Scotland. The tower portion of the church dates back to the 13th century. Families across the American South such as Dickson, Morris, and Marshall have distant kin buried here.

church structure. Whereas Luther wanted to retain the episcopal hierarchy of the Roman Church, Calvin believed the 1st-century Church provided the blueprint for structuring an efficient governance system that called for the election of elders (presbyters) and deacons from the congregation. The elders and deacons were responsible for providing leadership and ministerial support to the laity. They were also charged with the responsibility of electing a teaching elder (pastor). In Catholicism, the laity did not have any say in church matters or in the selection of priests. Knox believed that Scotland was in desperate need of these teachings and a nationalized church government to replace the ineptly administered and theologically flawed Roman Catholic Church.

After a thousand years in Scotland, the Catholic Church had amassed a huge fortune in properties and rents, while the peasants suffered hardships. Scotland's location on the periphery of Europe and far from the feeble oversight of Rome made the Church in Scotland especially guilty of abuses and contradictions. The Catholic Church had little impact on Celtic behaviors. Forrest McDonald describes the Celts of Wales with some help from Giraldus Cambrensis, who chronicled the Welsh for King Henry II in 1185:

> "[The Celts] do not live in towns, villages, or castles, but lead a solitary existence, deep in the woods." . . . They loved music and were skillful at it. They were an oral people, having a bardic tradition and being "endowed with great boldness in speaking and great confidence in answering. . . . They love sarcastic remarks and libelous illusions." They were sexually of loose morals. They were "very sharp and intelligent," but they "rarely keep their promises, for their minds are as fickle as their bodies are agile."

According to Leyburn, "by the middle of the sixteenth century Scotland was in a lamentable state. It was the Catholic apologist [defender of the faith] Hilaire Belloc who affirmed that the corruption of the Church, which he characterized as very bad everywhere throughout Europe in the sixteenth century, was worst of all in Scotland." Owen Chadwick goes on to suggest that Europe's lamentable condition can be well understood in the context of what he calls four contradictions in the Roman Catholic Church.

The first contradiction centered on the Bible as the source of truth. For centuries, the Church had taught doctrines that were not supported in scripture. Because few people then could read in the vernacular, let alone in Latin, the contradictions went relatively unnoticed. By the 1460s, however, spurred by the advent of printing presses and a general rise in literacy, contradictions between Church teachings and scriptural text became increasingly evident. Doctrines like the veneration of Mary and the saints, the belief in purgatory, and prayers to aid the dead were obvious departures from scripture.

The second contradiction that caused the decline of Roman Catholicism in Scotland involved the power of the Church as an economic force. According to Leyburn, before the Reformation the Church in Scotland held a monopoly of power, wealth, and influence. He states, "Its worldly might was evident in material form, for by 1560 it had amassed, through donations and wills, property estimated to consist of more than a third of all the land in the country and half of its wealth. In politics it was certainly a power to be reckoned with."

The Church failed in creating an image consistent with the poverty and long-suffering of Christ. Though there were feeble parish schools, a few universities, understaffed hospitals, and nuns and friars who had taken vows of poverty, the abundant wealth of the Church, which was mostly held in lands, rents, farms, houses, and woodlands, struck a discordant note with the people. The fact that the Church was a strong ally to the Stewart dynasty also added to its power, while it outraged the enemies of the royalty.

The third contradiction involved the idea that the Church was an instrument of peace. In its early years the Church had

Jedburgh Abbey in ruins. Scottish Borderlands. After the Scottish Reformation, ornate Roman Catholic abbeys such as this one were badly neglected. Many were stripped of pictures, statues, and any icons the reformers deemed idolatrous.

not wished its members to fight. However, as the religion spread and more of the population of Europe embraced Christianity, it was simply not practical to restrict Christians from the practice of war. There were times, in fact, when fighting was the Christian thing to do. For example, in A.D. 732 Muslim armies marched through Europe's Iberian Peninsula and over the Pyrenees Mountains into the Frankish kingdom (in the location of modern France), but they were stopped at Tours by a Christian army led by Charles Martel.

On the British Isles and the European continent, government and the Church were always connected. Because the Pope, aside from his duties as the leader of the Christian religion, was primarily concerned with his security, he required money and an army to defend his Italian stronghold. Even though the Church taught the importance of turning the other cheek, Christian kingdoms were expected to protect their religion on the battlefields of Europe and beyond, a result of the symbiotic relationship between the Church and the royalty that governed the kingdoms.

According to Chadwick, "Many people did not mind the sight of popes at war; it was part of man's fallen state, and if there are times when war is morally right it could not be wrong for a pope to be in a war. But other people felt that this broke a commandment of Jesus. To maintain its system, the Church had to be militant, in the military sense of the word." The Roman Catholic Church's contradictory stance on war was a significant factor in its declining hold on the Scottish people.

The fourth contradiction concerned the notions of celibacy and fidelity. The law of the Church restricted clergy from marrying. By 1550, however, a number of priests were openly living with women, even having children, which further discredited the Church in Scotland.

The contradictory actions of the Roman Catholic Church and its clergy led many Scottish people to seek an alternative. The political and economic power of the Church, however, made finding another option a difficult task. When news of John Calvin's Protestant Reformation reached Great Britain, people took notice. Some, like John Knox, saw Calvin's teachings as the perfect replacement for Roman Catholicism. Calvin's teachings, however, could not be implemented until the Roman Catholic Church relinquished its privileged position in Scottish society and politics.

Reformation Comes to Scotland

Many Christians in Scotland wanted to reform the Church and rid the country of its corrupt practices. No reform could happen, however, without the help of the nobility, who were concentrated in the comparatively more arable Lowlands. From 1542 to 1561, Scotland was ruled by regents, including the widowed queen consort of Scotland's King James V, Mary of Guise. Mary of Guise was a native of France. As the mother of Scotland's next monarch, who was yet a child, Mary decided to send her daughter, who was also named Mary, to France, where her family raised her as a Catholic.

At home in Scotland, Protestants were at work early in the regency to gain the support of the nobles. Over the next 19 years, a political and religious power base was formed in the Lowlands in opposition to the Catholic Church, which was a rival landholder to the nobles in southern Scotland.

John Knox, who had earlier in his life been imprisoned for his anti-Catholic views, went into exile in Geneva, where he learned much of his theology and church governance ideas from John Calvin. By 1559, Knox had assumed the leadership role in creating a Protestant Reformed Kirk. The reform ideas of Knox gained tremendous support among the Lowland peasants and nobles, but the Gaelic-speaking Highlanders did not embrace Knox or his Protestant reforms. With the support of the nobles and peasants in the Lowlands, the Scottish Parliament banned the Latin Mass on August 17, 1560.

Scotland had gone through many changes while Mary was in France. When she returned to Scotland in 1561 to assume her role as queen, she was already the widow of a young but sickly king of France. Mary had chosen to spell her name *Stuart* instead of *Stewart*, which was the practice in France. Despite her physical beauty and charm, she knew little about Scottish culture, for she had planned to rule Scotland from Catholic France. This, of course, caused great alarm in the Scottish Lowlands, where the Reformation and nationalism were already deeply rooted.

After the death of her husband, King Francis II of France, Mary lost the title of queen consort. She was left with little choice but to return to Scotland. Her youthful age, ignorance of Scottish culture, and overreliance on physical charms caused her to make bad political decisions, including speaking and writing in French to English and Gaelic constituents. Her devotion to Catholicism also did little to help her gain favor and support from Scotland's Protestant nobles and Church leaders.

It did not take long for conflict to grow between the Catholic queen and John Knox over his goals to create a state that was pure and Christlike and, of course, Protestant. The state would be modeled after Calvin's Geneva. Knox was so impressed with the way Calvin exerted control over Geneva in the name of the Church that Knox described the city as "a perfect school of Christ."

The way in which Mary handled her personal life destroyed her reign as queen and any hopes of the return of Catholicism to the Scottish Lowlands. Mary was married three times during her short life. She was implicated as a coconspirator in the death of her second husband, Lord Darnley, the father of King James I of Great Britain. In the minds of pious church leaders and protestant nobles, Mary's guilt was galvanized when she quickly married a primary suspect in Darnley's murder.

Mary was forced to abdicate the throne, and when she went into exile in England, she was placed under arrest. In 1587, evidence surfaced that Mary was planning a Catholic revolt in England. Queen Elizabeth, who supported Mary's son, the Protestant King James VI of Scotland, had her executed. All hopes of a resurgence of Catholicism in Great Britain went to the tomb with her, and the Protestant Reformation in Scotland and England was well on its way.

Though the Scottish Reformation was complete in relation to the end of Roman Catholic Church dominance, the subsequent struggle in the Protestant Church focused on structure and control. As early as 1572, James VI's regent, the Earl of Morton, made attempts to change the structure of the Kirk to an episcopal model that featured monarchial control. This struggle grew worse during the reigns of King Charles I, the Cromwell Protectorate, and the Stuart Restoration under Charles II.

The resulting military conflict over church structure and control actually became a contributing factor in the migration of Scots to Ulster, especially after the Scots were decisively defeated at the battle of Bothwell Bridge in 1679. This topic will be dissused in greater depth in the next chapter.

Presbyterianism and Limited Democracy

The Scottish Reformation ended an ineffective religious system and replaced it with one that blended well with the bleak landscape of the Lowlands and the fatalistic view of its people. The new era brought unity to Scotland, even though the Highlands were still largely Catholic. Imprisonment was the lot for those caught practicing the Catholic faith. Nonetheless, the Lowland peoples were a nation again, the first time such a condition prevailed there since the days of Wallace and Bruce.

The unity and continued revival were brought about by three interrelated conditions. The first reason was attributable to the clergy, who were educated and interested in ministering to the people. No longer were the clerics guilty of the old corruptions. The attention appealed to the people because most were peasants and had never been highly regarded by anyone. Now they attended church with nobility and may have actually worshiped next to them during services.

A second reason was created by the Kirk's insistence on education. Parish schools were established, and any young lad who felt led to enter the ministry could do so with the blessing of the Kirk. The Calvinist theology of the Kirk focused on the individual and his or her relationship to God. To have a relationship with God, the parishioner would have to know God. The only way a person could become intimate with God was through His spoken and written Word.

A third and powerful reason for unity and continued revival in Scotland was due to the presbyterian system itself. Each congregation elected a session to govern it. The session sent representatives to the presbytery, and the presbytery sent representatives from its body to the general assembly. In the context of the Kirk, the people had a voice.

The voice of the people was heard only if it did not represent dissent, however. Those who committed heresy were executed. A good many people suffered at the hands of neighbors who suddenly became zealous crusaders against sin.

The Role of Education in the Kirk

Despite the establishment of parish schools to supply educated young men to the four major universities in the land, poverty and a void in the scholarly world persisted in Scotland. Universities were located at Aberdeen, Glasgow, Edinburgh, and St. Andrews. Before the Reformation, Scotland's economy and political condition were so poor that there was little wealth to devote to learning the arts. When the Renaissance swept through Europe, Scotland was left out. Even in the religious realm, there were no Scots of the stature of Patrick or Columba. Scotland was simply a poor country on the periphery of Europe. Despite the availability of education, cultural practices that were developed over many centuries of insecure existence kept economic change in Scotland in check.

The Kirk did away with art and ornate rituals in worship services, though there were a few abbeys that boasted fine art. Church life resembled everyday life, in that neither offered any visual relief from the long, dark winters. Education's purpose was to prepare believers for an intimate relationship with God, not to entertain them. The instruction offered to the youth of Scotland was geared toward theology, not toward science and the arts as in other Western European countries. Churches built after the Reformation were simple structures with little resemblance to the ornate abbeys of the Catholic Normans. As the next chapter shows, these practices were imported to Ulster and the American South.

Religion in Ulster and the American South

@@@

Prior to the reign of James I, it was the policy of Tudor monarchs to either exterminate the rebellious Irish or to force them to adopt English culture. Neither Queen Mary's plantation in mid-Leinster nor Queen Elizabeth's more ambitious efforts in Munster achieved their goals. James I believed he understood the principal reason for the failure of his predecessors' attempts to Anglicize Ireland. The king reasoned that the Tudors' efforts to solve the "Irish problem" of rebellion and backwardness failed because there simply were not enough English settlers.

For centuries, English settlers, including Normans, had assimilated into the dominant Irish population and had become part of the so-called problem. When he ascended to the English throne in 1603, James enthusiastically inherited the Tudors' scheme to anglicize the native Irish. The Plantation of Ulster was a project that he attacked with intense personal interest, declaring its objectives "worthy always of a

Ulster-American Folk Park, County Tyrone, Northern Ireland

Christian prince to endeavour." The king was already experienced at trying to settle Catholic areas with Protestant colonists. From 1597 to 1607 he tried unsuccessfully to plant Protestants in Kintyre and on the Isle of Lewis. The establishment of permanent Scottish settlements in Ulster was the direct result of the experience and wisdom of the king himself. The hard work of Sir Arthur Chichester, a dedicated English Puritan and Lord Deputy of Ireland, was an important aid to James and the enabler of Puritan ministerial recruitment in the Church of Ireland.

From 1610 to about 1633, the Church of Ireland, a branch of the Anglican Church with the King of England as its head, recruited Scottish clergy to fill ministerial roles in its Ulster parishes. The Covenanting Party was formed in Scotland to convince Charles I to stop his tyrannical methods of rule over the Kirk. One of his methods included forming an Irish Catholic army to help his cause of absolute authority. Because of increasing trouble in England and a loss of support in Scotland among the nobility, the king had to abandon his plans,

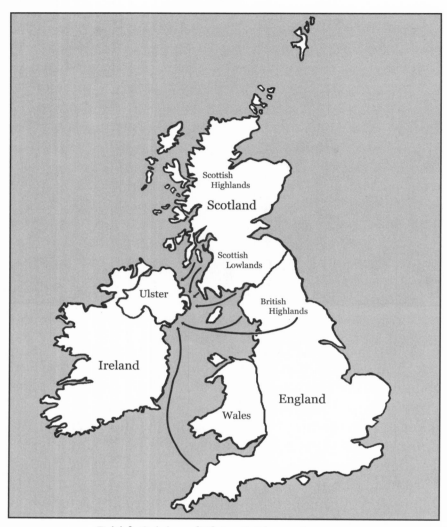

British Origins of Ulster Settlers, 1609-1717

but the Irish army he created remained intact. With the help and leadership of the remaining Catholic nobles who wanted an independent, Catholic Ireland, the army attacked Ulster Protestants.

The Scottish Covenanting Party sent an army to put down the rebellion. Among its troops were ministers. A number of the army chaplains created the first presbytery in Ireland on June 10, 1642, at Carrickfergus. It consisted of five ministers and four elders. Despite setbacks in Ulster such as the Catholic Revolt of 1641, the relative freedom of worship in Ulster kept the fires of revival going. The fuel for that fire came from the population of oppressed Lowland Scots.

Ulster was part of Ireland. Although Ireland had its own parliament, it did the bidding of the English monarch. Religious, economic, and environmental problems, as well as political factors, combined to cause the first great migrations to America in 1717-1718.

Early migration to Ulster from Great Britain was primarily for economic reasons. As the monarchy tried to impose on Scotland an Anglican church structure and order of service, Ulster remained remarkably free of restrictions for Presbyterians. To King James and perhaps to his successors, the issues of church order and governance were not related to theology and doctrines. James admired the High-Church style of the Anglican service and wanted to have his kingdoms observe the same religious rituals as a means for unity and control. As the 17th century progressed, religion replaced economics as the primary reason for relocating to Northern Ireland.

When James returned to Scotland in 1617, after an absence of 14 years, he brought Anglican churchmen dressed in white robes and his own edited version of Knox's hallowed *Book of Common Order*. Scottish Presbyterians were aghast when he tried to cajole and even intimidate them into adopting Anglican practices. The Scots never complied with James's order to change their manner of worship. James always seemed to know just how far he could push the Scots, so the issue remained at a stalemate for the remainder of his life and reign.

James's son Charles lacked his father's wiliness, and he set about to break the stalemate with the Scottish. Under Charles I, who ruled from 1625 to 1649, the Kirk was told to replace Knox's somber and simple order of service with High-Church Anglican rituals, commonly called the Laud's Liturgy. For both patriotic and religious reasons, the people overthrew the episcopal system in 1638.

Early Ulster schoolhouse

According to tradition, the spark that ignited the church revolt was struck in 1637 during a service at St. Gile's Cathedral in Edinburgh. A woman named Jenny Geddes, who was in attendance at the service, became enraged by what she thought was a return to Catholicism. As the High-Church rituals proceeded in stoic fashion, she "threw her stool at the head of the Dean conducting the service, shouting as she did so, 'Traitor, dost thou say mass at my lug [ear]?'"

In 1643, Presbyterian ministers and Puritan leaders in England negotiated a document called "The Solemn League and Covenant." The Covenant pledged to provide mutual defense against all enemies, to purge the land of popery, superstition, prelacy, and profaneness, and to support the privileges and rights of the Parliament to meet with the authority of the king. Although Charles disliked the Covenant, he subscribed to it.

Nonetheless, civil war broke out in England, with Oliver Cromwell and the Puritans hoping the Scots would join them in the fight against the king and his cavalier supporters. Scotland was divided over the idea of going to war against its Stu-

Early Ulster schoolhouse

art king, despite their disdain for his measures. When the king was executed in 1649, the Scots profoundly disapproved of the action.

Under Oliver Cromwell's Protectorate and the Stuart Restoration that followed, the strife in Scotland between royal forces and the Covenantors created martyrs for the Presbyterian cause. It also led to a massive migration of Scots to Ulster.

As it was during the reign of King James, the monarchy wanted a uniform church that could be easily managed. While religious practices in Ulster went relatively undisturbed for the dissenting Presbyterians, the Roman Catholics were dispossessed of their lands and deprived of a role in local government. Charles II implemented an annual payment to the dissenting Protestant churches of Ulster as a reward for their loyalty. The payment was called the *Regium Donum*.

Under Queen Anne, who ruled from 1702 to 1714, High-Church Anglicans gained control of Parliament, and the Test Acts that had been used to suppress the Catholics in Ulster were used against the Presbyterians. In 1703 the entirely

Protestant Parliament of Ireland, a puppet for the English government, voted to extend the Test Act to include all faiths that were not part of the apostolic succession. Interestingly, the provision recognized the validity of Catholicism but not Presbyterianism. As the 17th century neared its end, environmental, economic, political, and religious events converged on Ulster Presbyterians with such force that thousands decided to risk their lives in pursuit of the freedoms America offered.

When looking back on these events, Americans often take certain political and religious values for granted. For example, separation of church and state prohibits the government from showing a preference for a particular religious expression. It is said that the value was first championed in America by an English immigrant named Roger Williams, who established a colony at Providence, Rhode Island, in 1636.

Originally, the concept applied only to specific Christian denominations, but in recent years it has been generalized to all expressions of faith. At any rate, in 18th-century Ireland and Great Britain it was an alien concept. With the churches of Scotland and England existing as state institutions, it is possible that their actions during the 17th and 18th centuries set the stage for people to join other denominations when and where the opportunity presented itself. The backcountry of Appalachia was such a place, and the 18th century was such a time.

Liberty Beckons

As we consider the role of the Irish Presbyterian Church (IPC) in the events that led to the tremendous loss of its adherents, we must keep in mind that many circumstances faced by settlers in the New World were beyond the ability of any European church body to effectively address. We must also recall that there are an estimated 15 million Scotch-Irish and less than 4 million Presbyterians in America. The events leading up to the exodus from Ulster may provide some explanation for the decline of the IPC's ability to retain its followers once they reached the New World.

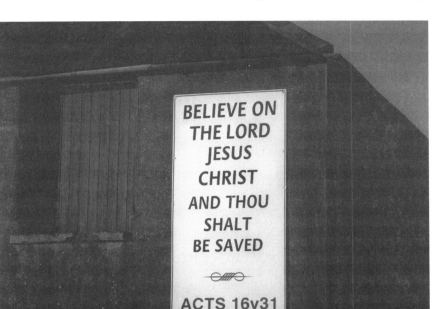

This sign is on a building in Ulster. Religious displays such as this are common in the American South.

Toward the end of the 17th century, the absentee landlords of the Ulster Presbyterians had accumulated tremendous debts. They expected to pay creditors with money from their rents. Most leases lasted for 31 years, and when they were up for renewal, the landlords doubled the rents, an act called *rack-renting*. The impact of the rent increases was devastating to the small farmer, as well as to entire communities. Dispossessed native Irishmen who eagerly wanted to own their land once more were able to gather together several kinsmen, pool their resources, and bid on land forfeited by Presbyterians. Many Presbyterians left Ulster for America, while some returned to Scotland.

The IPC remained politically silent during the rack-renting years. In contrast, many Anglican Bishops sought Parliamentary support for the protection of English woolen interests. Their effort partly led to the passage of the Woolens Act of 1699, which prohibited the sale of Irish wool and woolen cloth to all places except England and Wales.

In 1703 the British government passed the discriminatory Test Act, which required all officeholders, whether clerical or civil, to take Communion in the established Anglican Church. The Test Act effectively made the IPC's power in Ulster nonexistent. Pastors who remained true to the Presbyterian Church could not conduct weddings or funerals. Leyburn tells us that government authorities would delay funerals until the family allowed a rector from the Anglican Church in Ireland to conduct the services. Marriages that had been performed in the IPC were considered invalid. Those couples that were married in the IPC were considered to be cohabiting. A number of couples were arrested for this "sin."

The Test Act did nothing except alienate a valuable component of the provincial population. The Ulster Protestants had always supported the English monarch, perhaps out of tremendous respect for King James I. With the Act of Union in 1707, the Scottish government officially united with England. The union of the governments came on the heels of the Test Act. There is no doubt that many staunch Presbyterians in Ulster felt abandoned and vulnerable. The trickle of emigrants leaving for America would soon become a flood.

From 1699 to 1717, Ulster Presbyterians faced numerous hardships. They were subjected to smallpox epidemics, faced with a disease that attacked sheep, victimized by political decisions that damaged their woolen industry, and forced to endure a protracted drought that decimated the flax crop, which provided material for the successful linen industry. They were also treated as third-class citizens by the British government, especially in respect to their religious practices. Perhaps the final blow came when their parent nation, Scotland, joined in union with the tyrannical English government.

Considering the cooperation between the Church and the governments of Great Britain, it is not difficult to imagine that the Ulster Presbyterians felt abandoned by the Church, when they actually had been slighted by the government. The IPC

Fields of the Wood near Murphy, North Carolina. Among other things, Fields of the Wood claims the world's largest Ten Commandments, New Testament, and cross. It is a popular attraction for faithful tourists.

was silent throughout most of the tumultuous years leading to the exodus. As Leyburn writes:

> The Presbyterian Synod at first determined to stand by the defendants who resisted the [Test] Act, but they were soon dissuaded—and by financial arguments. The Regium Donum, that annual grant from the government which Charles II had bestowed upon non-conformist clergymen in Ulster in recognition of Protestant loyalty, was suspended. Presbyterian businessmen, fearful of a revival of animosities in Ulster if too great an issue were made of the Act, threatened to withhold their contributions to the Church. It seemed wise, therefore, to make the necessary submission and hope for lenient administration of the Act, despite its indignities.

To devout Calvinists within the IPC who wanted the Church to set the moral agenda for the state, the Church's submission to the British government did not seem practical. What the Calvinists wanted was a theocracy like the government that had been established by Calvin in Geneva, Switzerland. Nonetheless, early Presbyterian emigrants took the gospel of the IPC with them to the New World. In 1683, a Scotch-Irishman named Francis Makemie established the first Presbyterian congregation in America, on Maryland's eastern shore. When the first wave of Ulster immigrants arrived in the colonies, they were spiritually hungry. The Presbyterian Church in the British colonies tried to meet their needs, as the Kirk had done in Scotland.

Backcountry Evangelism and Presbyterianism

Upon settlement in the colonies, the Ulster Presbyterians were called Protestant Irish, Irish, or Scotch-Irish, and their interests were directed toward finding a niche in the new land. They were highly mobile. Their frontier character was forged in the borderlands and in Ulster, so they did not hesitate to move to the backcountry, where land was plentiful. The Pres-

Presbyterian church, Lancing, Tennessee. The humble style of the church reflects the beliefs of its parishioners

byterian Church had a difficult time keeping up with them, for not only were they mobile, they were also prodigious breeders.

While it is probable that a good many Scotch-Irish people left the Presbyterian Church because of geographic or logistical factors that separated them from Sunday services, it is also possible that many left because of their experiences with the IPC in Ulster. Let us not forget that Presbyterianism as a social institution may be conducive to the Scottish culture, but it is not an ethnic religion. According to Rubenstein, an ethnic religion is associated with a specific group. For example, Judaism is an ethnic religion, and those who are Jews, according to their faith, believe they are the chosen people by virtue of their biological connection to Abraham.

Universal religions, on the other hand, have tenets that make them attractive to many cultures. As "God's chosen in Christ," the Scots reformers believed they were among the adopted seed of Abraham. It was their belief that God had predestined them for salvation "before the foundation of the earth." They did not believe this favored condition, however, was based upon being Scottish, Irish, or even Presbyterian.

In America's backcountry, the belief in Presbyterian theology was often carried on without the supervision of the Church's governing body. Over the decades and centuries since the American Revolution, variations of the pioneers' Calvinistic understanding of the relationship between God and humans can be found in many of the denominations of the South, especially in certain Baptist sects.

The Presbyterian Church was not solely concerned with evangelizing the Scotch-Irish. In fact, America's largest Presbyterian denomination, the Presbyterian Church in the USA (PCUSA), has 2.5 million members. Seven percent of its members belong to racial minority groups. Those who are white likely belong to a variety of ethnic groups. Smaller but growing Presbyterian denominations like the Presbyterian Church in America are more homogeneous with respect to ethnicity and race. They are also more conservative and Calvinistic than their larger, more mainstream sister denomination.

In earlier chapters, we discussed the marriage of Anabaptist Germanic men and women to Scotch-Irish spouses, so we will not elaborate on those unions here, except to say that there can be little doubt that their religious systems were mixed in the rugged and isolated backcountry. The Germans and the Scotch-Irish shared fundamental Christian beliefs. Those beliefs are expressed in the Five Points of Calvinism, which explain the human condition and our relationship to God. The five points of Calvinism are:

Total Depravity
Unconditional Election
Limited Atonement
Irresistible Grace
Perseverance of the Saints

It is helpful to note that the first letters of each word form the acronym TULIP. Total Depravity tells us that humans are unable to save themselves from damnation. Unconditional Election is the belief that God chooses His elect based on His own will and that humans can do nothing to earn salvation.

Limited Atonement refers to the belief that some people will not be chosen for election (salvation), although some modern Baptists believe that this limitation is due to God's foreknowledge. They argue that God can see into the future and knows who will accept His offer of salvation. He efficiently does not call those who He knows will reject Him.

Irresistible Grace rests on the principle that God is sovereign and that no one can resist His offer of salvation. Like the story of Jonah and the great fish, people can try to flee God's plan for their lives, including election, but God will act through natural means to get them on the right track. *Perseverance of the Saints* ("once saved, always saved") is a doctrine that rests on the eighth chapter of the Book of Romans, in which it is written that nothing can separate God's elect from the love and salvation of Christ.

By 1738, the views of Jacobus Arminius, a Dutch Reformed theologian, were widespread in Western Europe, but they had not yet reached America. His views, which became known as Arminianism, attacked the foundation of the Five Points of Calvinism. According to Arminian notions about salvation, human free will is inconsistent with unconditional predestination and irresistible grace. The belief rests on the notion that humans have the God-given ability to reject the Holy Spirit and God's offer of salvation. The Arminian doctrine has continually inspired great speakers and spiritual songwriters to work hard to win souls to Christ.

During the 1730s, a movement within the Anglican Church embraced Arminian beliefs about free will. The movement was led by the powerful and inspiring evangelical work of John and Charles Wesley. In 1738 their efforts gave birth to the Methodist Church. The Methodist mission to the American colonies was led by the tireless travail and fiery sermons of George Whitefield and later Francis Asbury.

Whitefield made several trips to the colonies and preached to the common man. He traveled from the outposts of Georgia to the villages of New England, helping to spread the Great Awakening as he went. Religion to him was of such consuming importance that nothing else mattered. He made vivid God's love, the reality of sin, the agony of hell, and the bliss of heaven. Creeds did not concern him; the condition of a man's soul did. Wherever he went, whether in towns or in the backcountry, he drew enormous crowds that hung on his every word.

The power of the Methodist movement rested on the idea that humans have a choice concerning their eternal destination. Pastors then set about to present sermons designed to effect an emotional reaction to the ideas surrounding heaven and hell, salvation, and the love of Christ. Once the individual was emotionally sensitized to the reality of hell, it was thought, he or she would easily choose salvation by accepting Christ as a personal savior. In the backcountry, this idea became wrapped up with the perceived workings of the Holy Spirit. To the backcountry worshiper, it was the Holy Spirit that convicted the sinner's heart, not the frightful words of the preacher.

The ideas of Calvinism seemed much colder and impersonal than those espoused by the Arminian circuit preachers. Fearing an even greater loss in membership, the Presbyterian Church split into two camps—the Old Siders and the New Siders—in 1745. While it is not fair to say that the New Siders were Arminians, it is accurate to say they respected the evangelical fervor of the Great Awakening (the religious movement that swept the colonies in the early 1700s) and wanted their church to be a part of it. The Old Siders were more conservative and wanted to retain many of the religious rituals of Ulster and Scotland.

The New Siders were willing to be less formal and therefore were considered to be "low churchmen." The New Siders, however, were committed to high standards of education for the clergy and were responsible for building the College of New Jersey, which later became Princeton University, and many of the earliest colleges in the South. The Old Siders, despite their conservative nature, opened an American seminary called Newark Academy.

Church historians have provided us with this interpretion without an awareness of the revivals that were common in Northern Ireland. In her book *Triumph of the Laity: Scots-Irish Piety and the Great Awakening,* Marilyn Westerkamp shows that the Scotch-Irish brought revivalism with them from Ulster.

The debate within the Presbyterian Church was short-lived. Unlike the conflict in the Scottish Lowlands in the last half of the 17th century over the imposition of Anglican High-Church ways on Presbyterians, no blows were thrown and no shots were fired between the Old Siders and the New Siders. Leyburn says, "The bitterness of dissension that divided the Presbyterian Church gradually abated, and by 1758 the breach between Old Side and New Side was formally healed. . . . Neither side had won, but the church that came together in 1758 was considerably different from the church that had split in 1745." The major change in the church was the merging of the of Irish, Scots, Scotch-Irish, and English ethnic factions into an institution composed of Americans.

The efforts to change and minister to a free and rapidly expanding American population could not keep up with the Baptist congregations that ordained a man as a minister under a simpler requirement: spiritual calling to the office.

In fact, many ordained preachers in the Baptist Church could not read. They relied heavily on oral culture to learn scripture and doctrines. Baptist preachers, unlike their Presbyterian counterparts, did not have to deal with synods and bishops. They worked only with the congregation, and many of the members were often kin and lifelong friends. This factor, however, cannot explain all of the increasing denominational diversity among the Celts in the colonial Upland South.

Forces of Diversity in the Southern Church

The number of adherents in the various Presbyterian denominations has declined as a percentage of the Scotch-Irish population. For example, in the middle of the 18th century, one could reasonably assume that nearly all of the Scotch-Irish were at least nominally Presbyterian. Today, however, less than 18 percent are. This inflated percentage reflects an assumption that all white members in the Presbyterian community are Scotch-Irish. Perhaps the greatest reason for the decline of Scotch-Irish membership in the Presbyterian Church during colonial days rests with the rugged remoteness of Scotch-Irish settlements in the backcountry. Leyburn argues that seminary-educated clergy were reluctant to relocate to such places when more attractive opportunities to fill pulpits were available in Scotland and Ulster.

For those young men in the backcountry who felt called to preach, their choice of pulpits was extended beyond those of the Presbyterian Church. The Scotch-Irish lad had more choices in church affiliation than did his Lowland Scots ancestor, who had only the Kirk. Choice, however, was not the only factor that created denominational diversity in the South.

There are two basic reasons for the appeal of backcountry Christian meetings among Celts on the frontier. The services were culturally and personally appealing. One viewpoint argues that Celts are a creative people with a strong oral culture that encourages stirring stories, lifting music, and vivid expressions of material art. Circuit-riding preachers inspired by the oratory of the evangelists who led the Great Awakening gave the Celts fiery camp meetings and spirit-filled revivals.

It is likely that most of the backcountry folk, as well as their Lowland Scots ancestors, appreciated a good and stirring story. Let us explore the oral culture of the Celts. McDonald, writing in McWhiney's book *Cracker Culture: Celtic Ways in the Old South*, provides ample evidence of the bardic orientation of Celtic culture. Lively and descriptive sermons would have fit the bill for a story-loving people.

Certainly most Celtic people also appreciated music, but some thought music, when set to hymns, was not biblical. In the wake of the Reformation, the same stark logic applied to the presentation of icons in many northern European houses of worship. The American frontier allowed the Celtic orientation toward emotionally appealing music and sermons to assume a greater role in the religious lives of the Scotch-Irish than the austere, education-demanding services provided by Presbyterian ministers, including the progressive New Siders.

Flynt and Leyburn provide us with a second opinion on the appeal of camp meetings and revivals. Flynt writes, "Both yeomen and poor whites attended, but the lack of economic and social mobility among the poor was the key to understanding revivalistic appeal. Within the sects, members could achieve some measure of control over their lives and some degree of status."

Leyburn notes, "By modern standards they preached inordinately long sermons, to people who had seldom heard discourses from the pulpit but now seemed to hang on every word. One is almost persuaded that the intellects of the Scots had never before been stirred and that the preachers for the first time made humble folk feel their own dignity and worth." Leyburn seems to think that the sermons were an uplifting experience for the spiritually deficient, including those who had some measure of wealth. It is worth noting that spirit-filled services may have been sponsored by any number of denominations or by independent groups.

The Calvinist doctrines of the pioneers have been somewhat diluted by Arminianism and are found in many Baptist churches today, including the Primitive, Regular, and Missionary denominations. Even the Southern Baptist Convention, which is the largest Christian denomination in America next to the Roman Catholic Church, shares many doctrinal positions with Calvinists.

Other Reasons for Diversity in Celtic Christianity in the South

The process of decline in the Presbyterian Church was caused by more than stylistic reasons related to culture and personal esteem. Freedom and bad memories, interaction with Germanic peoples, and a departure from Calvinism are presented as further explanations for ecclesiastical diversity among the South's Celts.

First, when we recall that the Scottish Kirk's name was, in Anglicized form, the Church of Scotland, it must be entertained that the Kirk had a monopoly on church attendance in the Lowlands, and those who chose to go to the Roman Catholic Church were severely punished. Perhaps freedom of choice empowered backcountry families to attend services with other congregations.

Second, the presence of German neighbors sensitized the Scotch-Irish immigrants to the sacrament of adult baptism. Another, and more tenuous, factor relies upon the Celtic predilection for an oral and musical culture. Baptist and Methodist services were highly emotional, and little, if any, reading was expected from the congregation. Successful pastors, in true Celtic fashion, were always animated and entertaining.

Third, the Cumberland Presbyterian Church, established to fulfill a desire among the Scotch-Irish to ordain non-seminary graduates, was founded in 1810. The Cumberland Presbyterians wanted to de-emphasize the doctrine of double predestination, which states that God not only predetermines who goes to heaven, but also those who will go to hell.

In 1801, a man named Baron Stone ignited an attack on the Westminster Confession at Cane Ridge, Kentucky. The "Westminster Confession of Faith" is the Calvinist document used in the Presbyterian Church to proclaim its faith and teachings. Today, the Westminster Confession is still used among conservative Presbyterian denominations. The revival Baron Stone started among Presbyterians led to the formation of the Disciples of Christ denomination.

Denomination Affiliation Today

Religious diversity in the South is clearly reflected in the numbers of denominations across the land. It was not always that way. For example, in terms of the number of pastors working in America in 1776, the Presbyterian Church was the fourth-largest Christian denomination. Of all the ministers in the states, its pastors represented only 10 percent of the total.

In the Middle and Southern States, however, the Anglican Church had the most pastors, with 54 percent. At that time, there were more Presbyterian ministers than there were Baptist preachers in the South. In fact, 22 percent of all the pastors in the South were Presbyterian ministers, and only 18 percent were Baptist affiliated.

Over time, the Presbyterian Church has moved away from its ethnic roots, and Celts have become important and integral parts of other churches in the South. One fact is clear, however—most of the descendants of the original Scotch-Irish and Anabaptist Germans have remained true to their ancestors' theological positions.

Table 4 shows the changes in Baptist and Presbyterian attendance with respect to other denominations:

Table 4
Attendance Ranks for Denominations in America

Denomination	1750	1820	1850	1995
Baptist	6	1	3	2
Catholic	8	9	9	1
Congregationalist	1	4	7	9
Disciples	N/A	5	6	7
Episcopalian	2	6	8	6
German Reformed	7	7	5	8
Quaker	3	8	10	10
Lutheran	5	4	1	4
Methodist	N/A	2	2	3
Presbyterian	4	3	4	5

Note that these data reflect national trends over time, and that only the largest denomination in a category is included. In other words, numbers on the Presbyterian Church membership in 1995 are taken from the PCUSA, and they do not include, for example, data on the Cumberland Presbyterians.

With respect to Table 4, the Presbyterian Church has not held its own, placing in three decreasing ranks (3rd, 4th, 5th). The Baptist Church, however, moved from 6th place in 1750 to 1st in 1820. Today, only the Roman Catholic Church exceeds the Baptists in number. Other denominations, such as the Congregational Church and the Quakers, have lost tremendous ground to the congregations that developed during the Great Awakening.

In the Upland South, Tennessee in particular, the Presbyterian Church has not fared well in attracting adherents. According to Kennedy, Presbyterianism is the fifth-largest category of Christian churches in the state. The Baptist Churches have 1.6 million members. It is the largest denominational category in the state, followed by the Methodist denominations, with 419,000 members. The Church of Christ, with 219,996 members, and the Roman Catholic Church, with its 137,202 adherents, are also larger than the Presbyterian category of denominations.

Of the 132,344 Presbyterians, over half belong to the Cumberland Presbyterian Church, and a good many others belong to the conservative Presbyterian Church in America (PCA). Assuming Tennessee is representative of the region, it is apparent that the PCUSA has failed to effectively evangelize in the Upland South.

Celts and Religious higher Education

Today, all major Presbyterian and Baptist denominations support certain colleges and universities. For example, the Presbyterian Church in the USA convenes an organization called the Association of Presbyterian Colleges and Universities (APCU). The Association has 67 member schools. Of that number, 61 percent are located in the South or on its periphery. Table 5, on the following page, shows the PCUSA-affiliated colleges and universities that are located in the region.

Table 5
APCU Colleges and Universities in the South

School Name	State
Stillman College	Alabama
Lyon College	Arkansas
University of the Ozarks	Arkansas
Eckerd College	Florida
Agnes Scott College	Georgia
Centre College of Kentucky	Kentucky
Lees College	Kentucky
Pikeville College	Kentucky
Belhaven College	Mississippi
Mary Holmes College	Mississippi
College of the Ozarks	Missouri
Lindenwood College	Missouri
Missouri Valley College	Missouri
Westminster College	Missouri
Barber-Scotia College	North Carolina
Davidson College	North Carolina
Johnson C. Smith University	North Carolina
Lees-McCrae College	North Carolina
Peace College	North Carolina
St. Andrews Presbyterian College	North Carolina
Warren Wilson College	North Carolina
University of Tulsa	Oklahoma
Beaver College	Pennsylvania
Grove City College	Pennsylvania
Lafayette College	Pennsylvania
Knoxville College	Pennsylvania
Waynesburg College	Pennsylvania
Westminster College	Pennsylvania
Wilson College	Pennsylvania
Presbyterian College	South Carolina
King College	Tennessee
Maryville College	Tennessee
Rhodes College	Tennessee
Tusculum College	Tennessee
Austin College	Texas
Schreiner College	Texas
Trinity University	Texas
Hampden-Sydney College	Virginia
Mary Baldwin College	Virginia
Davis and Elkins College	West Virginia

In addition to the colleges listed in Table 5, there are other schools in the South that have Presbyterian affiliations or Reformed traditions. The college for the Presbyterian Church in America, the second-largest Presbyterian denomination in the United States, is located at Lookout Mountain, Georgia. Its name is Covenant College. Erskine College in South Carolina is affiliated with the Associate Reformed Presbyterian Church. The Reformed Theological Seminary campuses in North Carolina, Florida, and Mississippi are also important schools associated with Scottish Presbyterianism.

Scotch-Irish Presbyterians founded Washington and Lee University in Virginia, as well as the colleges that became the University of Tennessee at Knoxville and the University of Georgia. The Cumberland Presbyterians support Bethel College, which was founded in 1842 and is located in McKenzie, Tennessee.

Despite the denomination's frontier orientation toward spiritual beckoning and revelations though dreams and other paranormal means, Baptists in the South have embraced higher education in a liberal arts context. A few of the institutions that support higher education and training for Baptist clergy and lay people are: Liberty University in Virginia; Belmont College in Tennessee; Baylor University in Texas; Mississippi College, Shorter College, and Mercer University in Georgia; Oklahoma Baptist University; Ouachita Baptist University in Arkansas; Campbell University in Kentucky; and Southwestern Baptist University in Missouri.

The Methodist Church, which traces its origins to the tireless work of Arminian preachers within the Anglican and Episcopalian congregations of England and Virginia, has a long tradition of educating clergy. Some of the more prestigious Southern institutions of higher learning affiliated with the Methodist and Wesleyan denominations are: Duke University in North Carolina; Vanderbilt University in Tennessee; Emory University and Berry College in Georgia; Southern Methodist University in Texas; Southern Wesleyan University in South Carolina; and Bartlesville Wesleyan in Oklahoma. These are just a few of the powerhouse institutions that blanket the Southern landscape with liberal arts educations that are supported by teachings from the Wesleyan tradition.

Superstitions, Apparitions, and Premonitions

⊚⊚⊚

In the chapters on religion we discussed how the major strains of Protestantism came to the Upland South, as well as some of the forces that have shaped the rise and fall of certain denominations. It is tempting to assume that most Christians in the South have a familiar association with the theological bases of their religious beliefs. Though that assumption may be true for many, there are a number of Christians who unwittingly carry with them Old World ways regarding superstitions, apparitions, and premonitions.

It is interesting that many members of Fundamentalist sects may be among those who unwittingly embrace extra-biblical notions that border on the paranormal. Folks such as these, who are often geographically isolated and poor, are demonstrating a link to the past. Most of the denominations in the South were once sects without overarching governing bodies and thus relied upon emotional evidence to support their beliefs.

The attitudes that support the existence of the supernatural are similar to the beliefs that were common among the Celts in pre-Christian Europe. The ideas that support beliefs in extra-biblical supernaturalism are preserved like other aspects of culture. As David Hackett Fischer informs us, intelligent back-country people had no better system for explaining the uncertainties of the secular world. A backcountry woman captures the essence of this notion:

> Speaking for my own people, I am sure that almost everyone has had some experience he cannot explain away. Perhaps he has heard a warning of someone's death, a strange noise, a shriek on the roof. Perhaps a man has passed him in the open road and disappeared suddenly, leaving no tracks. . . . My people, like the Hindoos and Scotch Highlanders, have the faculty of dealing with the occult, of seeing and hearing that which is withheld from more highly educated minds. Always there is some souvenir of the spirit world in a nook of the mountaineer's brain. He is unwilling to accept it, never believes quite all that it seems to imply. Still, there it is.

The poorest of the poor are likely to receive an oral, family-based, traditional education focused on life in the community. The combination of sect-like views, poverty, and limited access to higher social positions has preserved many Old World ideas that support extra-biblical supernaturalism. In many ways, people in lower social positions, regardless of their geographic location, are convinced their lives are governed by luck or other forces beyond their control.

The Celtic Roots of Southern Supernaturalism

Strong states that the Celts of the pre-Roman era were "dominated by the supernatural in the form of the spirits of woods, rivers, sea, and sky. Religious rites and ceremonies took place in sacred groves in which, when the gods were angry, propitiation was offered. . . ." The Druids, who were drawn from the noble class, were the Celts' intercessors with the spirit world. They used charms, magic, and incantations to deal with the gods.

To support the notion that pre-Christian supernatural traditions made their way to the American backcountry, let us pose some questions to ourselves. Have we ever heard of a haunted house? Have we ever heard of a leprechaun? What about four-leaf clovers? How about Merlin the Magician? In southern England, there is a place that holds the fascination of millions of people the world over. It is literally a collection of large rocks sitting on the rolling Salisbury Plain. There is no artistic value in them, except for the circular pattern that is formed by their positions. They have no clear meaning to anyone of this modern age, yet Stonehenge is a tourist magnet.

Perhaps it is human nature to marvel at the unexplained. The supernatural is an acknowledged part of life for a large portion of the people living in rural areas of the Upland South, but most do not recognize the pre-Christian origins of their attitudes about superstitions, premonitions, and apparitions.

This chapter shows the continuity of supernatural ideas in Appalachia with the Celtic lands of north Britain. The so-called problem of the Scots' involvement in the supernatural was so common in Scotland that in 1563 Mary, Queen of Scots, signed a bill, authorized by Parliament, to prosecute witches. A witch was anyone who performed charms, claimed the ability to see into the future, or was associated with any other manifestation of the supernatural not ascribed to the will of God. King James was so convinced of the presence of witches that he wrote a book on how to discover and punish them.

While Americans remember the Salem witch trials and think they are unique or unusual occurrences, Scotland in the 17th century tried much harder to stamp out superstitious behavior. Some 30 years after the death of King James, hundreds of people who were guilty of having a premonition or a visitation from a spirit were tried by the Kirk and condemned to death by burning.

Two witches were burned in the small Perthshire village of Dunning. In the nearby town of Auchterarder, one woman was burned as a witch after she simply walked by a man while he was working his cattle. One of his animals became ill and another died of sickness within a few days. It was believed that she had placed a hex on the beasts.

A few miles to the south of Dunning, in the village of the Croock of Devon, a dozen people, including a man, were tried and burned as witches. The trials were held in 1662, and twelve of the thirteen defendants were condemned to death. The lone survivor was found guilty but was not executed because she was pregnant at the time of her trial.

When it comes to ghosts, hauntings are big business in Scotland. Cities such as Edinburgh offer ghost walks in the evening hours. Places and structures that have any connection with celebrities from Scotland's past are keen to promote them as part of the local scene. They are popular with both locals and tourists.

In the backcountry of Appalachia, the supernatural ideas of the old country are still believed by many. The Kirk and the transatlantic journey could not eradicate the temptation to explain the unknown forces of nature with superstitious notions. The stories in this chapter reflect the persistence of this Celtic folk tradition.

All the stories in this chapter were provided by members of the communities of Sandy Gap in North Carolina, Oliver Springs in Tennessee, or Miami, Oklahoma.

Superstitions

My Scotch-Irish, French Huguenot roots run deep in Southern Appalachia. I grew up under the watchful care of my maternal grandparents, seeing, hearing, and tasting a world I took for

Maggie Walls Monument. In 1657, Maggie Walls (spelled *Wall* at the base of the monument because the "artist" ran out of space) was burned as a witch on this spot. The name Walls is common in the South.

granted. East Tennessee was the center of the universe as far as I was concerned. Since my youth, spent among family and friends pressed tightly together by the closeness of the deep valleys and rugged hollows, I have observed with amazement the evidences of Celtic settlement across the South. As a professor, college administrator, and researcher, I have lived in seven Southern states and in Scotland. I also lived in Michigan for several years, so I have also experienced the North's Anglo-Saxon-based culture. As I did when I was away at college, I still looked forward to trips home.

I recall a return visit to see my folks about 15 years ago. I felt the urge to rent a movie. After canvassing everyone in the home to find out if they had a preference, I grabbed my keys off the bar and darted out the door. Feeling youthful, I leapt off the wooden porch, passing my grandfather as he walked up the stairs. My juvenile action forced him to fix his attention on me. When I was about halfway to the car, I realized I was missing my wallet. I turned around and started back toward the house.

Pop yelled out to me, "Boy, whatcha thank yer doin'?"

"I forgot my wallet," I answered.

"Son," he replied, "don't chu know it's bad luck to turn around once you've started off somewhere?"

Suddenly I remembered my childhood instruction on how to avoid bad luck. I asked him if he would get it for me, and, of course, the loving and protective Pop fetched it.

Gardening at my family's home was also governed by the supernatural. Each year Pop would ask Nanny, my grandmother, if the signs were right for planting potatoes, corn, or beans. Pop's fishing habits were also governed by the supernatural. He would fish only on those days in which the signs were right.

Pop was convinced that the earth sits still in space and that the sun actually orbits about the world in a manner that is clearly rooted in theories of the universe that were in vogue during the Middle Ages. One of my fondest memories of him occurred when I was twelve years old. My uncle Cleo and I had debated Pop on the nature of the earth's orbit.

My grandpa was clearly not a theologian, but he steadfastly maintained his position by stating, "The Bible says the sun cometh's and the sun goeth's." When I told him that earth spins on its axis at just over a thousand miles per hour and that the seasons change because the earth travels around the sun while tilted 23.5 degrees, he laughed and shook his head.

"If we's a-movin like that," he said, "we'd fly ever' which a-way. Ain't no telling whar we'd end up." Tired and perplexed, we went to bed around midnight.

The next morning, my bald, round, and jovial grandfather joined Cleo and me in the kitchen, where he proudly announced that he had "got cold" during the night. With that said, he grabbed his belly with both hands and barked out with a hearty lift in his voice, "I reckon the earth slung me way up north through Detroit sometime during the night."

He died in 1995, never convinced that he had spent 82 years on spaceship earth. As this story illustrates, biblical and superstitious ideas frequently coexist with other peculiar notions that are rooted in beliefs that have their origins in Europe's Dark Ages.

The superstitious ideas associated with pregnant women are among the most interesting traditions I know. In rural Cherokee County, North Carolina, there was a lady named Elsie Craig, who was pregnant sometime during the war years of the 1940s. According to Vernedith Voyles, Mrs. Craig had an experience while visiting a friend that seems to validate a superstitious notion.

It was a beautiful day for a stroll along the mountain route that Mrs. Craig followed to her friend's house. The beauty of the clear blue sky and the absence of any traffic on the dry dirt road made the day seem as though nothing could possibly go wrong.

When Elsie arrived at her friend's home, her host had pulled a chocolate cake from the oven and had cut two pieces.

The cake was steaming, and the kitchen smelled like a fine bakery. Elsie wanted a piece of that cake so badly that she had to restrain herself, for she feared her ravenous appetite would make her look like a pig. She smacked her cheek so hard it left a red mark on her face. When her baby was born, it had a brown, crescent-shaped birthmark on its cheek.

Another backcountry woman experienced the supernatural while walking down a dirt road. It happened in Cherokee County, North Carolina, during the years of the Great Depression. The woman was in the first trimester of her pregnancy. She was walking down the road, apparently involved with her thoughts, and did not notice a large rattlesnake coiled only a few feet from her. When the snake rattled its tail, the pregnant woman jumped with fright. Her right hand landed with tremendous force on her right thigh. She hoped to frighten the reptile, but the snake continued its threatening rattle.

When she gathered her thoughts, she realized that the snake was just out of striking range. She was able take a few steps back and move to the other side of the road. Out of harm's way, she made it home safely. Like Elsie Craig, when this lady delivered her baby, the object of her emotional experience was emblazoned on the infant. The child had a birthmark on its right thigh. The mark formed a snakelike pattern.

Vernedith Voyles herself was victimized by this unknown but powerful force. In 1934, she and her mother, Sarah E. Payne, were hoeing corn in the mountains of Sandy Gap. Vernedith was pregnant, so her mother had come to help her in the fields. Her husband, Rufus Voyles, was out of the state, looking for work. With only themselves to care for the fields, the two women attacked their chores with resolve.

Trees lined the edge of the cornfield, and one of them was a healthy apple tree. Vernedith spotted a luscious, ripe fruit on one of the highest limbs. She stopped her work, walked over to the edge of the garden, and stood in the shadow of the tree. As her mother caught up with her, Vernedith said out loud, "I'd sure like to have that apple up thar."

Sarah recognized her statement as a request and said, "I believe I can reach it with ma hoe." Sarah was able to get the apple with her tool, and when she struck it, the apple came down so fast that neither woman could react in time to catch it. Vernedith tried to move out of the way, but the falling fruit slammed into the back of her head and neck. Vernedith's baby Dorothy was born a few months later. She greeted the world with an apple-shaped birthmark on the back of her head.

Children growing up in Appalachia are taught many ideas about luck and superstition. When they reach adulthood, they are sensitized and do not find them strange. As entertaining as these stories may be to a more sophisticated audience, they serve the people of the backcountry in many practical ways.

Some superstitious teachings are designed to control the behaviors of potentially wayward children. I recall being told this one—"Singing at the table, whistling in bed, Devil come and get ya by the hair of the head." I've yet to find that passage in the Bible. One of my favorite warnings to kids involves the infamous boogeyman. I still remember hearing, "You kids better get in this house. The boogeyman's gonna get ya." I never saw the boogeyman, but I knew if I ever did, my luck was gone. Umbrellas had the power to give us bad luck, but only if we opened them in the house. Also, "If a black cat crosses the road in front of you, bad luck is your fate." Of course, walking under a ladder and breaking a mirror were also reasons to expect bad luck. The presence of superstitious beliefs in the Upland South is beyond debate. The roots of these ideas are in the Celtic lands of Europe.

Apparitions

When I was growing up in Tennessee, I was certain of two contradictory things, though at the time I did not see their incompatibility. The first was that there was a God who loved me when I laid my head down to sleep, and the second was that I had better not venture into a dark room at night, because old man McTavish's ghost would be waiting for me. As the backcountry lady wrote about her people and their experiences with ghosts, most people in the South that I have met have either heard of instances in which a ghost revealed itself to someone, or they have experienced a sighting themselves.

I had my own personal experience with Mr. McTavish. One night I had begged my grandparents to let me sleep in the attic, thinking it was safe because Mr. McTavish and his wife had died downstairs. We had the kind of attic stairs that fold down from the ceiling. Once I was allowed to lay my weary eight-year-old head to rest in the attic, my loving grandmother folded the stairs up behind me.

The attic was a neat place. It was finished on one end, while the other half was still rough. There were two windows. The floodlights from outside provided ample illumination throughout the attic. As I lay in bed, I could and did survey the entire floor area. The area was clean of all apparitions, including Mr. McTavish and his deceased wife.

I had a transistor radio under my pillow to help me go to sleep. When I felt drowsy, I reached under my pillow, grabbed the transistor radio, and rolled over onto my back so I could place the radio on the nightstand.

My searching eyes found much more than the nightstand, for standing at the foot of my bed was a man dressed in a suit. He said nothing. He only stared at me. After I had adjusted my sight and realized that the man (the ghost of Mr. McTavish?) was still by my bed, I began to scream at the top of my lungs. I wasted no time in pulling the covers over my head.

Within hours (it seemed) I heard the stairs being lowered and the soft voice of my grandmother. I asked her if she had seen anyone, and she said no. To this day I believe I saw someone, but I am sure that I was conditioned to expect it.

In my community, kids would play outside until after dark in the summer. Sometimes parents would call nicely for their children, and, of course, their children would dutifully go home. Those who refused to go home would get the "boogeyman" routine. If that technique failed, some parents would dress up in a ghostly white sheet and work their way behind the unsuspecting kids. When the children became heavily involved in their play, one of the participating parents would jump out at the youngsters and scare them beyond belief.

In the chapter on order and violence we discussed Frank Voyles. Frank was a big, strong man. He frequently took on other people's fights, including the one that led to the shooting incident that left him partially paralyzed. In addition to Frank's physical size and powerful disposition, he had a soft spot for some people and their causes. As well, according to Frank's aunt Vernedith Voyles, he had "a wild streak in him." He liked whiskey, women, and song, which are traits of men in the Old South's Celtic culture.

Frank grew up in Sandy Gap. His mother and stepfather lived there all the days of their lives. In fact, most of the people who lived at the end of Cherokee County's Sandy Gap Road were Frank's relatives, including Vernedith and her two small children.

Frank reputedly had impregnated a local girl named Cary (an alias name). The girl was a few years younger than Frank, who was about 20 years old. She lived with her parents a mile or so from his family home on the back road to the Hiwassee river. Frank did not have a job and was too immature to take responsibility for a little baby and a wife. The couple broke up, and the young girl and her family prepared for the arrival of the baby. Clothes were made, toys were fashioned from local materials, and the girl's parents made room in the tiny log house for the infant's crib.

Frank, meanwhile, continued to make whiskey, drink it, sell it, and brawl with other local boys and young men. The nearest town of any size was Murphy, thirty miles away. Few men had cars to make such a trip, so social outlets for hedonistic men were found at the homes of friends or relatives, or in the woods. Sometimes men would gather outside churches and drink while the "good folk" went in for the service. Frank was the kind of man who would have stayed outside the church,

Early general store between the Hiwassee River and Sandy Gap, in Cherokee County, North Carolina.

drunk whiskey, and gotten into a fight. His mind was seldom on the young girl he had impregnated, let alone the baby she was carrying.

As it turned out, the young girl carried the child to term, but there were complications, and both the baby and the young mother died. The girl's parents were devastated, so they sold their house and land and left the area. The home sat vacant until it collapsed from decay. The new owners of the property were only interested in the timber on the land. After a few years, the land was sold to the US Forest Service, and today the land is part of the Cherokee National Forest.

Shortly after the land was sold to the Forest Service, Vernedith and her two girls, Dorothy and Ruth, were picking apples along the road to Hiwassee Lake. That day Vernedith heard someone walking toward her. She turned and saw Frank. He stopped long enough to tell her that he was going fishing. He had walked the four miles to the lake on a number of occasions, and today's trip seemed to be no different. It was a pleasant, late summer day.

Within an hour after Frank left Vernedith and the girls picking apples, he came storming back up the road from the direction of the lake. He stopped abruptly in front of the curious girls and a perplexed Vernedith. Quickly, he asked her if he could carry the young ones with him back to his mother's house. Before waiting for an answer, he had the two excited girls in the air, bouncing them on his shoulders as he walked. They were happy to get attention from their big cousin, but Vernedith knew something was amiss, because Frank looked terrified.

Vernedith finished her chores with the apples and went to gather her daughters at Bess Voyles's home. When she got there, Frank told her a frightening story. He said that he was making good time on his trip to the lake, but when he passed Cary's old place, which sat on a bank on the outside of a bend in the dirt road, he saw a beautiful young woman coming toward him.

At first he thought she was someone from down by the lake, and he even thought about asking her for a date. As he fixed his eyes on her, he saw that the girl was Cary. He stood frozen as the apparition moved to within a few feet of him. She was wearing a long dress, and her hair was hanging down to her belt line. She was beautiful, but dead. Frank watched her float several inches above the road as she slowly disappeared. Shocked beyond any experience he had ever had, Frank swore to his believing aunt that his story was true.

As is the case with superstitions, many folks in the Upland South are conditioned to accept strange events and their possible supernatural explanations. In the case of Frank Voyles, he probably suffered from a latent guilt complex associated with the death of the young girl and her baby.

When I was growing up, friends would entertain each other with ghost stories. I remember a scary one that was told to me and a group of friends the summer of my twelfth year.

On that balmy evening, my 18-year-old cousin, Mike Kannipes, told his very interested young listeners about a date he'd had with an old girlfriend and another couple. It was on a lazy, hazy East Tennessee night in the summer of 1972 when he found enough courage to ask Lori out for a date. His friends Pete and Sharon went along to help the childhood acquaintances get to know each other more intimately. Mike was very proud of his '56 Chevy, which featured a new red-hot paint job on its two-door hardtop body. A large-block V8 with headers and a manual four-speed transmission powered the car. It was every mountain boy's dream of a car that would impress girls.

Mike told us this story about his double date with Lori, Pete, and Sharon on a lonely gravel road that winds its way through the ridges and valleys of southwestern Anderson County:

We was in Oak Ridge, drivin' up the strip from Shoney's to McDonalds. We was gettin' bored, so I asked the girls if they wonted to ride out to Haney Hollow. They said "sure," so we drove on out that-a-way.

Then Sharon told Pete that he oughta tell Lori and me about the murder of a beautiful young Smith girl that happened way back down in Haney Hollow.

So Pete says, "Hey, y'all, pull the car over 'round that butt-kissin' curve up thar. We can find a parkin' place right next to that white oak tree on the right. Y'all ever hear 'bout that murder that happened up here 'bout thirty years ago? I wont to tell you'ns about that Smith girl that got kilt over in that field next to that old abandoned house."

Pete motioned with his hand for us to look out the window of the car to an overgrown field on the right side of the gravel road. We could see it plain 'cause the moon was a-shinin'. The moonlight was so bright that the old, abandoned house that sits over thar made a shadowy finger that looked like it was a-pointin' at us. We sat thar in the car, frozen stiff.

I didn't wont ever'body to know I was scared, so I calmly said "Let's get out." I told Pete to tell us about what happened to that Smith girl. All four of us got out of the car. I got a blanket out of the trunk for us to lay down on. I'm telling you what's the truth—we laid down thar on that blanket with the moon shinin' over that house, and I could have sworn that old porch was a-pointin' at us.

Anyway, Pete told us that his daddy'd told him 'bout how one day that cute Smith girl, I believe her name was Rita, was busy doin' her chores. It was in the mornin' when she went to bustin' kindlin' fer the cook-stove. Her ma and pa was over in the next holler, pickin' up walnuts or somethin', when this feller pulled up in a loud car. Her daddy told the police later that he heard a car revvin' up its engine. I reckon that got him to thankin' maybe he ought to go see what was a-happenin' at the house. He lit out a-runnin', but 'fore he ran 20 paces he heard three gunshots ring out.

When he got to the house over thar, his poor beautiful daughter was layin' in a pool of blood. Police said it looked like there had been an attempt to rape the girl, and she had grabbed an ax as she tried to get away from that guy. I thank her panties were ripped off or somethin' like that.

Anyway, she musta turned on the man and drew back to hit the feller, 'cause she lay on the ground with the ax still in her right hand. It was drawn back over her shoulder. Her other hand had two bullet holes through it where, I reckon, she tried to protect her face from the shots. Of course the bullets went through her hands and her head. Police said she was deader than four o'clock 'fore she hit the ground.

I told Pete, "Now, that's some bull." Then Lori got up and said she wonted us to take her home. I coulda kicked Pete in the teeth for that. I tried to calm her down and it took a few minutes, but I talked her into sittin' back down again.

Before long, Lori sat up on the blanket and weakly whispered, "What's that noise?" Man, she was gettin' purty loud. She pointed toward the woods next to the old house and said, "It's comin' from over thar next to that house. Hey, it sounds like somebody's walkin' through the leaves toward us."

Me, Pete, and Sharon sat straight up. Pete said he could hear the sound too. I jumped to my feet, screamin', "I hear it too!"

I reached in the car and turned on the headlights. When they came on, we all saw a beautiful young woman walkin' right toward us. She was carryin' an ax, and blood was drippin' off it. Then she drew her left hand up to her face, and in them headlights we could see her arm was covered in blood.

I'll tell you what—we jumped in that car and got the hell out of there. My wheels was a-throwin' gravel, and we fishtailed it back to Highway 61. I headed toward Oliver Springs without lookin' back.

Mike told his enthralled all-boy audience that the Oliver Springs police stopped him that night doing 130 miles-per-hour in a 25-mile-per-hour speed zone. As our older cousin finished his story, I could see goose bumps on his bare arm. It was 85 degrees that evening. He was terrified and so were we.

In the western foothills of the Ozark Mountains there is a region that stretches from near the Missouri-Arkansas border to southeastern Kansas and into northeastern Oklahoma. Many people in the region have reported seeing mysterious lights at night, but no one has unraveled the secrets behind the illuminations. In Ottawa County, Oklahoma, a light has been spotted in the farmlands east of Miami for over a century.

Some have speculated that automobiles or farm trucks traversing pastures at night cause the lights. Others look to the supernatural for their explanations of these events. As the

The author in the Ozark Mountains

descendants of Celtic pioneers moved westward, they took their explanations of the unknown elements in the natural world with them. One such explanation involves an apparition that cannot find solace.

Despite Hollywood's depiction of Oklahoma as a dry, rolling prairie, the eastern part of the state closely resembles parts of Tennessee, Georgia, and Arkansas. The ample rainfall supports a lush green natural habitat.

On a warm, late spring evening in the 1890s, the dark rich soil east of Miami was in the process of drying after a thundershower. The coolness of the night caused the moist air to

155

condense over the tiny farmhouses that dotted the landscape, resulting in a blanketing, damp fog. In one of those little farmhouses lived a farmer, his wife, and their teenage son. On this particular evening the farmer had gone to a nearby town to trade for a horse.

Because the storm had raged for over an hour, the young boy was not able to feed the hogs and bed down the horses before sunset. When the sound of rain hitting the tin roof stopped, the woman asked her son to "grab a lantern and slop bucket and go feed them animals."

The boy dutifully did as his mother had requested. After kissing her on the cheek, the lad opened the door and stepped out into the Oklahoma darkness. His mother smiled as he pulled the door shut.

Minutes passed into hours, but the boy did not come back into the dryness and comfort of his mother's home. The woman paced the floor as she asked herself over and over, "Where could he be?"

Just before midnight, she decided to take a lantern and look for him outside. She lit the oil lamp she kept in the cupboard and opened the door, hoping to see her son waving to her from the pigpen. *Maybe he found a snake and captured it for his pa to see when he gets home*, she thought. *He's always a-wantin' for his daddy to be proud of him.* Her longing eyes, however, did not find his silhouette by the pigpen, nor did she see him anywhere else.

When morning arrived, she was down by Tar Creek, looking along its banks. Still, there was no sign of her son. She spent her day visiting neighbors to see if anyone had seen him, but no one had. No one would see him again.

According to local legend, the woman spent the rest of her days losing her sanity as she looked over her farm for her lost son. She searched even at night. She carried an oil lamp as she struggled through all kinds of weather in her quest to find her lost child.

If you ever travel historic Route 66 at night through Ottawa

County, Oklahoma, you may spot a lonely light off in a pasture. It may not be a car or a truck. According to local legend, it might be a sorrowful mother in search of her lost son.

Premonitions

Just as the Bible is alive with incidents in which the future is foretold, so is the Upland South oftentimes imbued with ill-omened folk stories that thrill the listener or reader. I believe that most of these stories are simply examples of Celtic storytelling at its best, but there are other instances in which the persons involved earnestly believe that something happened that is beyond normal understanding. Thus, in their minds, there must be a supernatural explanation. The incidents I am about to share with you were told to me by people who are of good character and who believe they were the recipients of omens that revealed horrible events that were soon to occur.

The first event took place during May, 1939. Once again, the location is the mountainous community of Sandy Gap. Lewis Pankney Payne and his wife, Sarah, had raised ten children and were in the process of rearing two grandchildren. The nearest home to theirs was half a mile away.

Lewis and his wife were in their early 60s, but they still had to work to survive. Sarah tended the garden in the spring and summer, while Lewis assembled goods for his peddler business. He concentrated his efforts on peddler work because he had suffered a stroke and had lost the use of many of his motor skills. Fieldwork was simply too hard for him.

With summer drawing near, Lewis expected to sell quite a few goods, because the closest town was 20 miles away; therefore his wooden wagon filled with dry goods was always a welcome sight at the homes of people in northwestern Cherokee County. One of Lewis's grandsons, 13-year-old Arvil, helped him make his rounds.

One of their nearest neighbors was Lewis's daughter Edith and her husband. They were farmers and were looking forward to a bountiful year. One night, as the sun set over the Blue Ridge Mountains, Edith heard a whippoorwill singing its sad song. As the sky grew darker, the sound of the solemn night bird drew closer to their house. By bedtime, the bird had settled down on the tin roof.

The woeful sounds of the whippoorwill kept Edith awake. On several occasions she went out into the dirt yard and tried to scare the feathered pest away, but the spotted little bird would only fly up into the air a few feet, then settle back down on the roof to share with Edith the mournful sounds of its lonely song.

While Edith was contending with her winged pest, her mother and father were also doing nervous battle with a little bird that had never bothered them in the past. In fact, whippoorwills had always been a symbol of comfort to them, that is, if they came in small doses. Normally the birds would sing a soulful song in the evenings, and after about an hour their singing would stop. This night was different.

The next morning, Arvil and his grandfather readied themselves for their day as peddlers. They had breakfast, loaded the wagon, and hitched up a pair of mules. At sunup, the whippoorwill was still at its post on the roof of the house.

At this point, Lewis said, "That bird has done worn out its welcome." A broken garden tool was lying in the yard, so he grabbed it with his good hand and hurled it toward the bird. The tiny creature flew into the air for a couple of seconds, then settled back down on the roof and continued its unwelcome tune. Just after daylight, Lewis and Arvil left Sarah and the irritating little bird behind.

The mules pulled the load without strain. When they had gotten down the road a piece, however, Arvil says that "Pa pulled back on the reigns and bent over."

Concerned about the wagon's abrupt stop, Arvil asked, "What's wrong, Pa?" His grandfather seemed to be looking under the mules' bellies, but he wasn't. Lewis P. Payne was dead.

Perhaps he should have listened more closely to the whippoorwill.

Another ominous event that occurred in Sandy Gap reinforced the notion that animals have the insight to deliver warnings. This case involved the Rogers family, which included Amariah, Martha, Ann, and Bell (alias names). Amariah and Martha had built their wood-frame house by themselves. They cut the trees out of the woods that grew along the dirt road to the Hiwassee River and hauled the timber to McKinley Stiles's sawmill to be cut into lumber. They built their home in the clearing where they had removed the trees. It was the last dwelling on the road to the river.

In customary fashion, the family swept their new yard to keep out weeds and grass. Grass and other plants were hard to cut and trim without a lawnmower, so most of the people in Sandy Gap simply kept them out of their yards by sweeping them regularly.

The remote location of the home and its proximity to the Hiwassee River made the Rogers family popular with friends and neighbors who liked to hunt and fish. Felix, Amariah's brother, loved to hunt and would sometimes visit with the family for a while before heading into the woods to pursue game.

One summer evening, a terrible storm ravaged the mountains. When it was over, the western sky at dusk was alive with crimson and gold colors. Martha had just finished washing her youngest daughter's hair when she heard a horse galloping along the lake road. Amariah, who was lying on the couch, raised up and said, "That must be Felix a-comin' to go fox huntin', I reckon." The sound of the horse grew louder until it left the road and whisked past the porch, through the muddy yard, and into the dark forest. The family went out to see if Felix had fallen off the horse and hurt himself.

Felix was nowhere to be seen, nor was the horse. Once back in the house, the family talked about the rhythmic sound of the horse's gallop and wondered whose horse could possibly have gotten out and made its way to their remote home. Early the next morning, Ann and Bell couldn't wait to get outside and find the hoofprints in the mud. Amariah and Martha soon joined them. A complete survey of their yard was made, and not one impression of a horse's hoof was found.

Martha and Amariah were dumbfounded. They decided to go around to each of their neighbors to see if anyone was missing a horse. If they found who was missing one, they could at least tell them the direction the horse was traveling. By noon, they had made the rounds. No one was missing a mare, a gelding, or a stallion. They returned home and joined the kids hoeing corn in the fields when Bell spotted Nell Voyles quickly walking toward them.

"Martha," Nell yelled, "you better come with me. Mr. Patton done fell off that purty horse of his." Martha wasted no time in getting herself together. Side by side, the women ran to Nell's house.

A near-exhausted Nell explained to Martha that Old Man Patton, who had been staying with them, was posing on his horse for a photographer when Mr. Patton suddenly, and without apparent cause, jerked back on the reins. The horse locked up its legs, causing its feet to dig into the ground. As it slid to a halt, the horse left furrows in the moist soil.

Mr. Patton tried to stop his forward motion, but he could not. The elderly man tumbled over the horse's head and struck the ground with a thud. Mr. Patton lay motionless on the muddy ground. He did not respond to Nell's efforts to revive him, so she panicked. When she was able to think rationally, she decided to get help from Martha.

When Martha and Nell reached Mr. Patton, his skin was clammy and his face ashen. Martha sat on the ground next to the old man and placed a wet cloth on his head. Martha said, "As I was lookin' at him, a dark shadow come up over his head. I reckon that's when he died. I believe the horse that trotted past our house last night was givin' us some kind of warnin' about poor old Mr. Patton's death."

Haunted Buchanan Castle. This castle is located near the bonny banks of Loch Lomond and Glasgow, Scotland

Martha Rogers's account of the events leading up to the day of Mr. Patton's demise shows a strong attempt on her part to explain how disparate events prove the presence of supernatural forces in their lives.

There is one explanation for the sound of the galloping horse that has never been advanced by anyone in my company. Here is my best attempt to explain it. On that night, the sky was clear, the air was calm, and the windows were open. I believe the family heard a large deer. Perhaps it was running away from a cougar or bear. My feeble theory could be wrong, however—no one found any deer tracks either.

Attitudes Toward the Environment

@@@@@@@@@@@@@@@@@@@@@@@@@@@@@@@@@@@@@@

Because Southerners of Celtic descent are likely to value a lifestyle free from government entanglements, which they consider a natural right, and desire a connection with the natural world, they do not often see the government as a proper instrument for preserving or conserving natural resources. In fact, they may not even view the environment as being in jeopardy. They also may be equally unaware of the hazards that exist to themselves or their children as a result of the mismanagement of forestlands, waste disposal, and the resultant contamination and sedimentation of waterways.

Celtic people have historically demonstrated a culture that values closeness to the land. Celts see themselves as masters of their environment, and the way they live in it helps them to preserve their liberty. Consider the words to Hank Williams Jr.'s song "A Country Boy Can Survive," in which the singer lives back in the woods with his family, dog, rifles, shotguns, and four-wheel-drive truck. His backwoods home is a place where he can raise "good ole tomatoes and make homemade wine" and "catch catfish from dusk till dawn," as well as being able to "plow a field all day long."

The song's lyrics epitomize the Celtic view of the good life, which extends back to the days when the Celtic world reached from Turkey to Scotland. Celtic people in pre-Classical Europe preferred a rural, backwoods life over an urban existence. The Celts who conquered Rome, for example, in the 4th century B.C. relinquished the city because they did not like urban life. They left Rome and went back to their tiny rural villages, just as many modern residents of Appalachia have returned from Detroit and other industrial cities.

When they were not at war, the Old World Celts were a pastoral people. The cool, moist climate in the British Isles is ideal for growing grass and other leafy plants. Sheep and cattle grazing became the dominant form of agricultural activity. Deep-plow cultivation was never well established in northern Britain, though peasants did grow vegetables on a subsistence basis. The same forms of agriculture were carried into Appalachia and the Ozarks.

The Cumberland and Ozark Plateaus are characterized by the deep hollows that are carved into the landscape. Because there is precious little arable land and extreme change in local elevation, few suitable building sites are available. As a result, homes are built in the flattest areas. These places are generally found alongside rapidly flowing rivers and creeks or in seasonally wet hollows, where temperature inversions during winter months represent serious health risks.

Firewood

The Upland South is the home of a people who relish activities that put them in competition with the natural world. For example, men enjoy outdoor sporting activities such as fishing and hunting. Few young men in the South have escaped pressure from their peers and male role models to bag an 8-point buck or reel in a 10-pound bass. Other activities are less combative, but they do gain the person a sense of "standing tall" over the natural world. Men and women alike enjoy bringing in crops of corn and potatoes or putting up dozens of cans of beans.

The felling of a large oak or hickory for firewood is an exercise of the individual's right to control the elements within his/her world. Securing firewood fits the Celtic notion of natural liberty. According to *Mother Earth News*, burning wood for heat connects one to the natural world just as harvesting crisp corn connects the gardener and bagging a season's worth of venison bonds the hunter. Eric Sloane, in his book *American Yesterday*, says, "Unlike a mess of oil or a heap of coal, a stack of wood is a living and gladdening thing to behold." In an old almanac it is written, "City homes are warmed by coal, but country hearths warm the soul."

The warmth from a wood-burning stove or fireplace can be quite welcome in the Upland South, because the region experiences marked temperature contrasts. In the summer the weather can reach the upper 80s, even the low 90s, but excessive and prolonged summer heat is rare. On the other hand, winters can be harsh and severe, resulting in potentially high heating bills. Because a good many of the Upland people are poor and are consigned to using expensive and energy-consumptive primary heating systems, they opt for a more convenient and inexpensive home-heating method as a supplemental source. Wood fuel fills that need.

Wood fires may be produced in stone fireplaces (with or without an insert), stoves, or furnaces. The newest wood-burning stoves and inserts are as efficient as electric heat pumps.

One might wonder to what extent wood is used for heating purposes. One study found that 40 percent of the rural households in Warren County, Kentucky, used wood as a heating source, compared to 16 percent in the city of Bowling Green. The proportion of wood-fuel consumers could be much higher if the country is subjected to a protracted energy crisis. The study also found that wood fuel consumption was inversely related to household income.

The difference in the proportion of homes that use wood for heating is attributable to the fact that most of the residences in rural areas are likely to be occupied by people who own the dwelling as well as the adjacent land. In most instances they have a ready supply of wood fuel. For various reasons, however, some households elect not to cut their own wood. Instead, they buy their fuel from a local source. Regardless of the method used to secure wood for fuel, burning it presents some potential health risks for those who use it.

In older wood-burning units, especially those that predate EPA regulations on emissions, wood is not completely oxidized. As a result, acrid fumes, particulate debris including polycyclic organic matter, carbon monoxide, carbon dioxide, and other non-desirable particulates are released into the atmosphere. If there is sufficient vertical air movement, these gases and particulate matter will simply disperse upward and eventually be moved away by upper-level winds.

Unfortunately, a significant number of the homes that burn wood for heat are located along creeks and in bottomlands. The chemicals and particulate matter in wood smoke are harmful to the human respiratory system. The situation is made worse at night when temperatures are usually coldest. People burn more wood after sunset, which releases more pollutants into the air. Also, temperature inversions often form at night because of the geography of bottomland areas.

Temperature inversions trap pollutants near the ground, where we readily breath them into our lungs. For example, after sunset, when wood burning is most intensive, cool air descends the surrounding hillsides, pushing aloft the warmer layer of air near the ground. When this happens, vertical mixing of air is halted, and the layer of warm air, which may be only 30 feet above the ground, forms a temperature inversion. The descending cold dense air effectively traps the pollutants emitted from chimneys and creates a health hazard.

Another problem related to wood-fuel consumption involves indoor pollution. In the Celtic realm, the materials used to ignite wood fires are even more toxic than the wood smoke. A number of people use empty two-liter bottles, milk jugs, or other plastic objects that would otherwise be discarded to ignite wood fires. As the door to the burning chamber, or fire-box, is opened, a draft is created. When the plastic is ignited, gases are released into the house before the firebox can be filled and the door closed. Since a completely filled firebox is highly desirable on a cold Upland night, the practice of filling it to capacity maximizes the time the firebox is open. Gases released from burning plastic are highly toxic and represent a health threat to those who live in the home, as well as to those who might be living near it.

During December 1989, many of the fireboxes in Warren County, Kentucky, remained hot, due to a protracted cold spell. Temperatures at night fell to as low as -9 degrees Fahrenheit, and the daytime highs remained below freezing. Water pipes froze in a number of homes, as did some that froze underground, away from the dwelling. It was a tough time. Energy consumption was so high that a good number of the homes that relied upon wood for heat went through their wood reserves in a matter of days.

Those who sold wood did well during the cold spell. As one might expect, price gouging occurred, and costs soared from $30.00 to $50.00 for a rick of seasoned oak. Seasoned oak burns more efficiently than wet oak, which emits a greater quantity of particulate matter and harmful gases.

I interviewed a man who sold wood during that time. He told me that he had sold just over 200 ricks during the month. The wood came from his family's properties in Simpson County. The wood supplied from this one purveyor amounted to 9,600 cubic feet. There were also a number of others selling wood at the time. According to Dr. Conrad T. Moore, who works as a biogeographer at Western Kentucky University, 200 ricks of wood is the equivalent of the annual growth on 4,000 acres of oak/hickory forest. The purveyor stated that he had no plans to reforest his family's properties. As innocent and wholesome as heating a home with wood may seem, the current system of supplying wood in the Celtic realm presents environmental problems not unlike those which decimated forestlands centuries ago in Celtic Britain.

Celtic people in the rural South are capable of changing in response to problems, but proposals to ameliorate those concerns must take into account their understanding of natural liberty. For example, replacing old wood-burning stoves with newer models might be a solution, but the people must be convinced that the newer models burn wood slower while producing similar amounts of sensible heat. Officials who approach them on the basis of environmental awareness will receive little more than a warm reception from the members of most rural communities in the Celtic realm.

The issue of reforestation will be even more problematic, because land ownership and management is deeply rooted in the notion of natural liberty. Of course, the National Forest Service offers free trees for fuel, a practice that is quite popular among the inhabitants of rural Southern communities. In Grenada, Mississippi, the National Forest Service and the State Forestry Commission have tree-giveaway programs. On the morning the trees are given away, the thousands allotted for harvest are usually gone within two hours of the opening of the event.

Clearly, any effort to improve an environmental problem in the Celtic realm must include ways to enhance the people's sense of natural liberty, and acquiring free trees certainly empowers that sense.

It's Our History Too

‌@@@

In recent years, there has been an explosion of heritage festivals across the South that allow Celts to gather and share their tastes for music, art, and stories. The Scottish Highland Games variety is very popular, because of people's interest in kilts, clans, and the beautiful Scottish landscape. Games are held during the warmer months of the year. The most popular Highland events, such as those held annually at Stone Mountain, Georgia, and Grandfather Mountain, North Carolina, attract over 100,000 visitors to their weekend activities. Highland games are also held at Radford, Virginia; Gatlinburg, Tennessee; Jackson, Mississippi; Glasgow, Kentucky; Montgomery, Alabama; Batesville, Arkansas; Arlington, Texas; Tulsa, Oklahoma; and Charleston, South Carolina. Many people who attend these games are keenly interested in genealogy, and Clan tents are set up to serve their need for information. However, despite the growing popularity of Highland festivals, many Southerners remain disinterested or uninformed about their heritage.

Europeans express amusement that Americans are so interested in their genealogies. Most Europeans are born, live, and

Stirling Highland Games. Tests of strength are important features of the Highland Games. This annual event in Stirling, Scotland, is held near the site where William Wallace's forces defeated the army of Edward I in 1297. Unlike Highland Games in the American South, Scottish games do not feature clan tents. In Scotland the emphasis is on events such as sheep dog trial, dancing, and tests of strength.

die in their ancestral lands. It is easy for them to take for granted the closeness of the places that played important roles in their histories. For example, at a small shop catering to tourists in Gretna Green, Scotland, a clerk told me that she thinks Americans are more Scottish than those who live in Scotland. She told me that she wears a kilt to work but never wears one away from the job.

At a restaurant in Bath, I had a long conversation with the lady who owned the adjoining inn. After I told her that some of my students and I were looking forward to seeing the border country from whence so many of our ancestors had emigrated, she laughed and said, "I think it is so fascinating how you Americans fancy that you are part of our history."

With a look of disbelief on my face, I advised her that, "We are, and you are part of ours." I explained to her that our history did not begin in 1776, or in 1492. I told her, "When Mary, Queen of Scots, was on her troubled throne and Elizabeth I reigned over England and Wales, our ancestors paid homage to them, for the queens were their sovereigns and your ancestors were their kin." The lady politely smiled at me, mirrored my look of disbelief, and went on with her chores.

Bibliography

Adams, Imagene. Interview by author, 2 June 2000, Murphy, N. C.

Atkinson, Jim, anthropologist and Dean of Continuing Education, Rogers State University. Interview by author, 12 July 1997, Claremore, Okla.

Bardon, Jonathon. *A History of Ulster*. Belfast: The Blackstaff Press, 1992.

Bell, Robert. *The Book of Ulster Surnames*. Belfast: The Blackstaff Press, 1988.

Birdsong, Jeff, political scientist at Northeastern Oklahoma A&M College. Interview by author, 18 February 2000, Miami, Okla.

Black, George F. *The Surnames of Scotland*. Edinburgh: Birlinn Limited, 1946.

Boettner, Lorraine. *The Reformed Faith*. Phillipsburg, N. J.: Presbyterian and Reformed Publishing Company, 1983.

Buchan, John and A. G. Smith. *The Kirk in Scotland 1560-1929*. Edinburgh: Hodder and Stoughton, 1930.

Burrell, S. A. "The Apocalyptic Vision of the Early Covenanters." *Scottish Historical Review* 43, no. 135 (1964): 1-24.

Campbell, John C. *The Southern Highlander and His Homeland*. New York: The Russell Sage Foundation, 1921.

Caudill, Harry M. *Night Comes to the Cumberlands: A Biography of a Depressed Area*. Boston: Little, Brown, and Company, 1963.

Caudill, Harry M. "Kentucky and Wales: Was Ellen Churchill Semple Wrong?" In *Cracker Culture: Celtic Ways in the Old South*, by Grady McWhiney. Tuscaloosa: University of Alabama Press, 1988.

Chadwick, Owen. *A History of Christianity*. New York: St Martin's Press, 1995.

Conlin, Joseph R. *The American Past: A Survey of American History*, 4th ed. Fort Worth: Harcourt Press, 1993.

Cummins, W. A. *The Age of the Picts*. Stroud, Gloucestershire, England: Alan Sutton Publishing Ltd., 1996.

Davies, Norman. *Europe: A History*. New York: Oxford University Press, 1996.

De Blij, H. J. and Peter OMuller. *Geography: Realms, Regions, and Concepts*, 8th ed. New York: John Wiley and Sons, 1997.

Dennis, Allen, history professor at Delta State University. Interview by author, January 1996, Cleveland, Mississippi.

Dickson, W. and E. W. Prevost. *Glossary of the Words and Phrases Pertaining to the Dialect of Cumberland*, 3d ed. London: Bemrose and Carlisle: Thurnam, 1899.

D'Souza, Dinesh. *Illiberal Education: The Politics of Race and Sex on Campus*. New York: Vintage, 1992.

Dunlop, John. *A Precarious Belonging: Presbyterians and the Conflict in Ireland*. Belfast: Blackstaff Press, 1995.

Durkheim, Emile. *The Elementary Forms of Religious Life*. Translated by Karen E. Fields. New York: The Free Press, 1995.

Durning, William and Mary Durning. *The Scotch-Irish Who Came to America: A Genealogical History*. La Mesa, Calif.: The Irish Family Names Society, 1997.

Ehrlich, P. R. and A. H. Ehrlich. *The Population Explosion*. New York: Simon and Schuster, 1990.

Falls, Cyril. *The Birth of Ulster*. London: Methuen & Co, 1936.

Fellmann, Jerome, Arthur Getis, and Judith Getis. *Human Geography: Landscapes of Human Activities*. Madison, Wis.: Brown & Benchmark, 1997.

Fischer, David H. *Albion's Seed: Four British Folkways in America*. Oxford: Oxford University Press, 1989.

Fiske, John. *Old Virginia and her Neighbors*. Boston: Houghton Mifflin, 1897.

Flowers, Alvin, former resident of Sandy Gap, Cherokee County, North Carolina. Interview by author, 12 August 2002, Dalton, Georgia.

Flynt, Wayne J. *Dixie's Forgotten Poor*. Bloomington: Indiana University Press, 1980.

Fraser, Antonia. *Mary, Queen of Scots*. London: Mandarin, 1997.

Fraser, George MacDonald. *The Steel Bonnets: The Story of Anglo-Scottish Border Reivers*. London: Harvill, 1989.

Giddens, Anthony. *Introduction to Sociology*. New York: W. W. Norton and Company, 1991.

Griffin, Patrick. "The People with No Name: Ulster's Migrants and Identity Formation in Eighteenth-Century Pennsylvania." *The William and Mary Quarterly* 58.3: 53 pars. 12 Sep. 2002

Harrison, Henry. *Surnames of the United Kingdom*. Baltimore: Genealogical Publishing Company, 1992.

Herm, Gerhard. *The Celts: The People Who Came out of the Darkness*. New York: St. Martin's Press, 1975.

Hess, Beth, Elizabeth Markson, and Peter Stein. *Sociology*. New York: MacMillan Publishing, 1992.

Hutson, D., former resident of Morgan County, Tennessee. Interview by author, 19 December 2000, Morgan County, Tenn.

Irish in America, The. Produced by Rhys Thomas. Greystone Communications, Inc. for A&E Network, 1997. Videorecording.

Johnson, James. *The Scots and Scotch-Irish in America*. Minneapolis: Lerner, 1991.

Johnstone, C. L. *The Historical Families of Dumfriesshire and the Border Wars*, 2d ed. Bowie, Md.: Heritage Books, 1994.

Jones, Dorothy. Former resident of Sandy Gap, Cherokee County, North Carolina. Interview by author, 11 July 1997, Oliver Springs, Tenn.

Jones, Gwyn. *A History of the Vikings*. Oxford: Oxford University Press, 1984.

Jubilee of the General Assembly of the Presbyterian Church in Ireland. Belfast: The Witness Printing Works, 1890.

Kearney, Hugh. *The British Isles: A History of Four Nations*. Cambridge: Cambridge University Press, 1995.

Kennedy, Billy. *The Scots-Irish in the Hills of Tennessee*. Greenville, S. C.: Ambassador-Emerald, Intl., 1995. Reprint, Londonderry: Causeway Press, 1995.

Kerbo, Harold R. *Sociology: Social Structure and Social Conflict*. New York: MacMillan Publishing, 1989.

Kurath, Hans. *A Word Geography of the Eastern United States*. Ann Arbor: University of Michigan Press, 1949.

Leyburn, James G. *The Scotch-Irish: A Social History*. Chapel Hill: University of North Carolina Press, 1962.

Luther, Martin. "Nifty-five Theses." In *A History of Christianity*, by Owen Chadwick. New York: St. Martin's Press, 1995.

McDonald, Forrest. Prologue in *Cracker Culture: Celtic Ways in the Old South*, by Grady McWhiney. Tuscaloosa: University of Alabama Press, 1988.

MacLysaght, Edward. *Surnames of Ireland*, 6th ed. Dublin: Irish Academic Press, 1991.

Magnusson, Magnus. *Scotland: The Story of a Nation*. London: HarperCollins, 2001.

Marger, Martin N. *Race and Ethnic Relations: American and Global Perspectives*. Belmont, Calif.: Wadsworth Publishing, 1985.

Martine, Roddy. *Scottish Clan and Family Names: Their Arms, Origins, and Tartans*. Edinburgh: Mainstream Publishing, 1996.

McKerracher, Archie. *Perthshire in History and Legend*. Edinburgh: John Donald, 2002.

McKinney, Gordon, director of the Appalachian Center, Berea College, Berea, Kentucky. Remarks made at the Northwest Georgia Crescent Meeting, 27 October 2000. Kennesaw State University, Kennesaw, Georgia.

McNeil, Robert. *The Story of English*. Produced by Macneil-Lehrer Productions and the British Broadcasting Corporation, 1986. Videorecording.

McWhiney, Grady. *Cracker Culture: Celtic Ways in the Old South*. Tuscaloosa: The University of Alabama Press, 1988.

Miles, Q. "The Spirit of the Mountains," in *Albion's Seed: Four British Folkways in America*, by David Hackett Fischer. New York: Oxford University Press, 1989.

M'Kerlie, P. H. *History of the Lands and Their Owners in Galloway*. Bowie, Md.: Heritage Books, 1992.

Moore, Conrad T., biogeographer, Western Kentucky University. Interview by author, January 1990, Bowling Green, Kentucky.

Parker, A. W. *Scottish Highlanders in Colonial Georgia*. Athens: University of Georgia Press, 1997.

Perceval-Maxwell, M. *The Scottish Migration to Ulster in the Reign of King*

James I. New York: Humanities Press, 1973.

Raitz, Karl B., Richard Ulack, and Thomas R. Leinbach. *Appalachia, A Regional Geography: Land, People, and Development.* Boulder, Colo.: Westview Press, 1984.

Ray, Celeste. *Highland Heritage: Scottish-Americans in the American South.* Chapel Hill: University of North Carolina Press, 2001.

Reid, A. G. *The Annals of Auchterarder and Memorials of Strathearn.* Perth, Scotland: Perth & Kinross District Libraries, 1989.

Robertson, Ian. *Sociology*, 3rd ed. New York: Worth Publishers, 1987.

Rose, Morris, owner of the Scottish Rose. Interview by author, July 1996, at Bahaylia, Miss.

Ross, David. *Chronology of Scottish History.* New Lanark, Scotland: Geddes & Grosset, 2002.

Rouse, Parke Jr. *The Great Wagon Road.* Richmond: The Dietz Press, 1995.

Rubenstein, James M. *The Cultural Landscape*, 5th ed. Upper Saddle River, N. J.: Prentice Hall, 1996.

Semple, Ellen C. "The Anglo-Saxons of the Kentucky Mountains: A Study in Anthropogeography." *Geographical Journal*, 1901. 17.

Shapiro, Henry D. *Appalachia on Our Mind: The Southern Mountains and Mountaineers in the American Consciousness, 1870-1920.* Chapel Hill: The University of North Carolina Press, 1978.

Sloane, Eric. *American Yesterday.* New York: Funk & Wagnalls, 1956.

Sloane, Verna Mae. "What My Heart Wants to Tell." In *Cracker Culture: Celtic Culture in the Old South*, by Grady McWhiney. Tuscaloosa: University of Alabama Press, 1988.

Smith, Philip D. *A Tartan for Me!*, 6th ed. Bowie, Md.: Heritage Books, 1994.

Smout, T. C. *A History of the Scottish People 1560-1830.* London: Fontana Press, 1998.

Sproul, R. C. *Faith Alone.* Grand Rapids, Mich.: Baker Books, 1995.

Strong, Roy. *The Story of Britain.* New York: Fromm Int. Publishing, 1996.

Teall, Gordon, and Philip D. Smith. *District Tartans.* London: Shepheard-Walwyn Publishers Ltd, 1992.

Tischler, Henry L. *Introduction to Sociology*, 4th ed. Fort Worth, Tex.: Harcourt Brace, 1993.

Todd, Lewis P. and Merle Curti. *Rise of the American Nation*. Orlando, Fla.: Harcourt Brace Jovanovich, 1982.

United States Bureau of the Census. *Statistical Abstract of the United States*, 116th.ed. Washington, D. C.: United States Department of Commerce, 1996.

Van den Berghe, Pierre. In *Race and Ethnic Relations: American and Global Perspectives*, by Martin N. Marger. Belmont, Calif.: Wadsworth Publishing, 1985.

Vann, Barry A. "Social Engineering in Higher Education." *The Christian Observer*. Manassas, Virginia, 1995.

Voyles, Euclid, resident of Cherokee County, North Carolina. Interview by author, 12 July 1997, Hiwassee Dam, North Carolina.

Voyles, Vernedith, former resident of Sandy Gap in Cherokee County, North Carolina. Interview by author, 14-15 July 1997, Oliver Springs, Tennessee.

Warmenhoven, Henry J. *Western Europe*, 5th ed. Guilford, Conn.: Dushkin/McGraw-Hill 1997.

Weber, Max. *The Protestant Ethic and the Spirit of Capitalism*. New York: Scribner, 1958.

Westerkamp, Marilyn. *Triumph of the Laity: Scots-Irish Piety and the Great Awakening, 1625-1760*. Oxford: Oxford University Press, 1987.

Williamson, Rev. Colin. Minister of the Stewartry of Strathearn, the Church of Scotland. Interview by author, August and September 2002, Aberdalgie, Scotland.

Wilson, John. *Dunning: Its Parochial History, with Notes, Antiquarian, Ecclesiastical, Baronial, and Miscellaneous*. Crieff, Scotland: Strathearn Herald Office, 1906.

World Almanac and Book of Facts. The World Almanac Education Group, Inc. New York: WRC Media Company, 2001.

World Almanac and Book of Facts. Mahwah, N. J.: Funk & Wagnalls, 1996.